WELCOME TO THE NUTHOUSE!

A Year in the Life of a Suburban Family

By
Peter McKay

Llumina Press

Requests for permission to make copies of any part of this work should be mailed to Permissions Department, Llumina Press, PO Box 772246, Coral Springs, FL 33077-2246

ISBN: 1-932303-10-3

Printed in the United States of America

To my wife Gretchen: the best friend I've ever had, the best wife I could ever have, and truly, the funniest person I've ever met.

AN INTRODUCTION, OF A SORT

This book is a collection of columns I wrote over the course of a year. The columns are about me, my beautiful wife, my wonderful kids, and my crumbling house. This part is not about any of those things, because it is just the introduction. The introduction to a book is supposed to tell you what to expect inside and let you know why the book was written in the first place.

I cannot tell you what to expect from this book. I have a pretty good idea that you will find some parts mildly amusing. Other parts may make you laugh out loud. If you take this book with you on summer vacation, you will probably find that the book will get full of sand, and may become soggy if you leave it on the beach chair and then sit on it after a swim. If you take this book out of the library, you will probably forget to bring it back in time, and then curse the book every time you see it on the bedside table, as it is now costing you five cents a day. If you loan this book to a friend because you loved it, with the thought that they will read it and enjoy it, you will never see it again, and not because it is so good. You will never see it again because people never return a book they have borrowed, especially when they have been told they just have to read it.

The only other thing I can tell you about what to expect from this book is that because it is a collection of individual columns, you can probably pick it up, flip open to any one page, and begin reading. In this way it is probably much like an L.L. Bean catalogue or Farmer's Almanac, and will probably end up in the bathroom with other books that don't require too much investment of time or attention. Eventually, it will get lost in a pile of magazines and catalogues, and one day will be thrown out by accident.

My first column came about only because one morning in the car my wife got tired of hearing me repeat the same touching (but tired) story of how my dad used to buy our Christmas trees on Christmas Eve. In a slightly exasperated voice, she said, "That's really great, why don't you write it down instead of just telling me?" Her goal, obviously, was to get a little peace and quiet on the drive in to town. Had she known that she was signing up for a lifetime of proofreading and editing those same stories, she might have opted for a more curt "Shut up, I'm listening to the radio."

In the end, though, I think I started writing because I imagined myself one day being old, tired and alone, with only memories to sustain me. Like many old people, I think that I will look back through the decades, longing for the days when my children were young, when I felt vibrant and alive. The kids will be off on their own, working in other cities as dentists, manufacturer's reps, tattoo artists, or car salesmen. It will be hard at that age to remember specific events clearly. I won't remember if it was Daniel or Jack who broke their arm in the tree, or whether Olivia or Catherine was the one who got pinched on the toe by a crab at the beach the year she was two.

I find myself often sitting back, say on Friday nights as we get pizza, or on a car trip, and saying to myself, "Capture this moment. Embed it in your memory. One day you will want to remember what made it all so special. This moment might just do it for you."

But because memories fade in time, and because I am already beginning to forget things that happened last week, let alone decades ago, I knew that holding things in my head was not enough. They have to be on paper. They have to be something that I can reach for as I sit in my chair by the fire. They have to be preserved so clearly that no matter how old I am when I read the stories, I will be transported back in time, living these events over again. For a few minutes, at least, my children will be innocent again, untouched by the world. I will be energetic and full of purpose, still able to determine the course of my life.

So in the long run, I don't care if you read it. If you're thumbing through it at a book store, put it back on the shelf. If you already bought it, I hope you saved your receipt. Because it's not for you. It's for me.

If, by any chance, you have lost the receipt, or you have taken the book into the bathtub and gotten the pages all wrinkly, or have put a cup of coffee on it leaving a ring, you probably can't take it back. In that case, you have my permission to read on. But remember, the whole time, that it is my story, that these are my memories, and that it is up to you to make your own and to hold on to them, in whatever way you can, for that day when you need them.

Welcome to the Nut House!

One of the reasons we moved to the suburbs 10 years ago was to give our children a chance to commune with nature. We'd been living in New York City and found that kids don't get much of a chance to ride bikes or run free if their parents are constantly scanning the area for homicidal maniacs. And we wanted our kids to be familiar with wildlife other than rats, which they affectionately called "New York squirrels."

While I have enjoyed the fresh air, I was not ready to deal with the animal population. There seemed to be an inordinate number of squirrels in the front yard when we first looked at the house, many of them eagerly trailing us as we walked the property. I almost tripped over one as I peered up at the gutters.

Once we moved in, I'd find one or two squirrels milling about on the front stoop every time I opened the front door. As soon as they saw the door open, they would dart around my feet, hopping against my shins, apparently trying to get into the house. Coming from the city, I found this extremely stressful. I was used to squirrels that ran away at the first sight of humans, and having one attempt to pry my feet apart to get into the house seemed a bit much. It got to where I was afraid to open the door, and would peer through a window to make sure the coast was clear before heading out for work.

As the weeks went on, they got more desperate and insistent. By the time I got the door open a crack, there were three or four of them twitching in anticipation. One actually made a full run for it and slammed into my shin, and I almost beheaded another as I slammed the door shut.

What made it more upsetting was that I had no idea why they were acting this way. They were clearly trying to get inside, but I had no idea what they would do once they accomplished their task. I pictured them careening around the house, knocking pictures off the walls, shredding cushions and hopping onto heads. I have always been uncomfortable around rodents (I can't even bring myself to pick up my son's hamster) and probably wouldn't be able to go to sleep if I knew yellow-toothed maniacs were prowling the house.

I finally resorted to kicking them each time I opened the door. (Before anyone gets angry, let me make it clear that I didn't have to kick all that hard. The average squirrel is so light they can go a good five yards with the slightest flick of your toe.) And while I admit I had the advantage in the battle, they all had razor-sharp teeth and quick moves. They were clearly not hurt by these furball field goal attempts, as they would simply hop up again and rush back to the door.

As the weeks went on, the squirrels seemed to catch on that they were not welcome in our house. (To be fair, they were also probably a little put off by my hysterical screeching as they jumped up on my legs.) They resorted to standing a few yards away, looking at me with their heads cocked to one side, each time the door opened. As time went on, they took less and less interest in us, and gradually returned to normal squirrel behavior (scrambling up and down trees, gathering nuts and getting run over by cars).

We later found that the previous owner had fed peanuts to the squirrels for most of the 80 years she lived in the house, and generations of squirrels learned to eat from her hand. As she got older and less able to take the weather, she left the front door open and sat in the front hall. The squirrels would scamper in, accept their daily ration of peanuts, and scamper out. Their puzzled looks, then, were entirely appropriate given that they were expecting peanuts and instead got a boot to the belly.

Through extensive research, I've found that the average life expectancy of a squirrel is about five years. Of course, this "average" is brought down by the many chuckleheaded squirrels who enjoy playing in traffic and subsequently end up as furry pancakes. But barring a squishing, a squirrel can live as long as 13 years. That means that there may be squirrels in my yard who still remember the peanuts and are simply waiting for their chance to make a rush through my door.

They better not try anything. I, in turn, haven't forgotten how to punt.

Canines Ripped My Jugular

I enjoy hearing from readers of my column. One of my favorite letters came from a woman who read my column at work during lunch, and snorted soda all over her desk.

When I write about dogs, however, the reaction is swift and unforgiving. I can say all kinds of sarcastic things about my wife, my plumber, my house and even my kids, but the minute I take on dogs, I have crossed a line. (One family wrote to tell me that I was simply a "horrible person.")

I don't argue with all those dog lovers out there. It's just that once you have seen a dog chewing on a piece of your flesh as if it were a stick of Juicy Fruit, you never look at the canine species again without a little suspicion.

My fear of dogs runs deep. When I was 6, we owned a black Lab. I can still see myself running, screaming, as the dog chased me through the house, intent on ripping out my jugular vein and feasting on my flesh. (My older brother had taught me that if a dog should bite me in the jugular, I would instantly become a veritable fountain of blood.)

Later, we owned a huge, shaggy Irish wolfhound, but I never thought of her as a dog. "Shannon" stood over 4 feet tall, moved slowly with a lumbering gait, and constantly groaned as a result of her arthritic hips. Her only real activity was wandering around the house looking for a comfortable place to rest her bones. Had she been able to stand on two feet she would have looked like an arthritic Wookie.

When I was 10, our neighbors the Andersons bought a black poodle named "Gin," a psychotic, whirling ball of flesh and teeth. As we played basketball outside the garage where Gin was housed, the dog would leap at the garage windows, scraping his fangs against the glass, leaving saliva streaks in his wake.

One day, Mrs. Anderson asked my mother to pick up some groceries for her because she was sick and unable to go shopping herself. My mother parked the station wagon at the curb and asked me to carry the groceries to the Andersons' door.

I remember the entire incident as if it happened in slow motion. I got out of the car and hoisted two brown paper bags into my arms. Mrs. Anderson stood inside her glass storm door. She was fumbling with her purse, pulling out dollar bills from her wallet. At her side, Gin jumped at the glass, teeth bared, the glass steaming. As I reached the halfway point in the lawn, the storm door flew open as the dog banged the latch. Gin bolted through the doorway, streaked to my right, and made a wide curve around the perimeter of the lawn. At first I assumed the dog was running away, as he seemed to be headed toward south Jersey.

I froze in fear as I watched the black fur ball with gnashing teeth pick up speed and circle back toward me. Gin was now arcing around behind me, on a direct course with my skinny, 10-year-old body. I turned toward the dog and held the groceries in front of me like a shield. Maybe if Gin were to hit a can of peas he would knock himself out, giving me a chance to run back to the car.

As Gin came within striking distance, he leapt into the air, clearly going for my jugular vein. I leaned forward, scrunching up my shoulders to protect my neck. Seeing no available jugular, the dog decided to take the next best cut of meat and sunk his teeth into my shoulder blade. I heard a horrible crunching sound as he bit a walnut-sized hole into my back.

I staggered forward in dramatic fashion, still holding the groceries. Mrs. Anderson ran up to me, a frantic look on her face. I held out the bags to her, trying not to faint. Out of the corner of my eye, I could see Gin continuing his loop around the lawn. The dog was no longer a threat, of course, because his mouth was full. As I slumped to the ground, it occurred to me that my brother had been right to warn me. It had taken a while, but a dog *was* truly feasting on my flesh.

So anytime I get a letter from some angry canine lover, I respond that I do indeed have a soft spot for dogs. It's about the size of a walnut, and it's on my right shoulder blade.

Picture Perfect

The other morning, we sent our twin 6-year-old daughters off to school for picture day.

We have not had good luck with school pictures. Our kids are beautiful (our vacation pictures come out looking like a Ralph Lauren ad), but they seem to have a hard time smiling naturally for the school photographer.

Last year was a bad one. None of those school pictures will ever see the light of day again. One of the twins came out looking fearful, as if the photographer had threatened her before clicking the shutter. The other just looked diabolical (The kid from "The Omen" had a sweeter smile.)

My 8-year-old son, with only one of his two front teeth in yet (and, of course, trying to show it off for the camera), looked like he ought to have a straw hat on and a pig under one arm. My 12-year-old looked much as he always does for school pictures -- constipated. And our oldest son, who managed to produce a somewhat natural grin, also happened to blink at the moment the shutter clicked. With his big smile and half-closed eyes, he avoided looking evil, opting instead for dumb and happy.

And with five kids all in school at once, it is sometimes hard to keep track of names, let alone picture-day schedules. We try to make sure on picture day -- if no other day -- that they will be neatly dressed and trimmed and that we have attempted to run a comb through their hair.

More than once, however, our kids have come home to innocently tell us that they had their pictures taken weeks earlier, and that it worked out well because they got to wear their favorite T-shirt or avoided a hair wash. The resulting pictures, with rumpled clothes and ratty hair, looked more like mug shots of juvenile delinquents than "Happy Memories." We have a drawer in our dining-room sideboard loaded up with bad photos of our kids, layer upon layer of creepy, sad and disheveled faces. We would just throw them out but I don't want to scare the garbage men.

So the other morning at breakfast, I sat for nearly 10 minutes with the girls, coaching them on natural smiling techniques. It was not easy, but I finally got them to where they could look comfortable and happy on cue. "Remember," I said. "Pretend like you just heard a joke!"

My own experience with school pictures was fairly traumatic. In the late '60s and early '70s, it was fairly common for boys to have long hair. Nevertheless, I was the only kid in my class routinely mistaken for a girl. (I wanted to look like a "hippie" but more closely resembled a young, brunette Jodie Foster.) When my fourth-grade picture came around, I wanted to make sure that I not only looked good but was clearly a male of the species. I got a fairly short haircut and dressed in a suit and tie. I smiled the most confident, manly, "Sears Catalog" smile I could muster and then awaited the results.

The day the pictures were handed out, my packet came with a handwritten note from the photographer. "We're sorry," the note said. "The negative was cracked, but we think the picture is still great!" I opened the packet and stared open-mouthed. The "crack" down the middle of the negative showed up in the photo as a long, jagged white line. The horrible part, though, is that the line ran directly from my left nostril down my chin and then along my brown suit jacket. I looked like a male, all right -- a male with an extremely long booger dripping out of his nose. The kids at my table gasped in horror, and I angrily stuffed the pictures back in the packet.

As we watched the girls get on the bus the other morning, I nervously called out to the twins, "Let's see those smiles!"

Standing side by side, they turned and grimaced at me, looking frighteningly like those creepy twins from "The Shining."

"No! Not diabolical!" I called out. "Natural smiles, remember?" They just started to grin bigger and bigger, until I could see more teeth than their pediatric dentist ever had.

"Girls!" I called out through the bus window. "Like you heard a joke! Like something's funny!"

The bus pulled away from the curb, and I sighed, knowing that the drawer in our sideboard was going to get just a little bit more crowded this year.

If Walls Could Squalk

This weekend, my wife is throwing a big family reunion at our house. She has rented a tent and hired a caterer, and invitations have been made and sent. One would think that all I'd have to do is show up, pop open a cold beer and make awkward attempts at mingling. Unfortunately, this party (like many others before it) means that I'll probably have to redo our entire house.

Before a big social event, some women panic at the last minute and change outfits at least five or six times. A friend who has been married for 40 years told me that when his wife starts stomping back and forth to the closet, changing clothes and wailing about how everything she has makes her look fat, he simply slips out and waits in the car with the windows rolled up.

My wife is pretty good about getting dressed. She does, however, have last-minute anxiety attacks about the shape of our house. Suddenly, slightly nicked woodwork becomes "disgusting." The kitchen cabinets, which I see as sort of homey and lived in, are an eyesore and must be repainted, if not replaced. What was once a nice red striped wallpaper makes our living room look like a "Christmas present in a cathouse."

The end result is that I am up till 2 or 3 in the morning the whole week before a big gathering, trying to make our house look as though it sprang from the pages of House Beautiful.

As the plans for the big shindig took shape, I sat by quietly in the background, hoping our house would make it to the party intact. My strategy in such situations is to begin talking up the house.

"You know," I'll say spontaneously and convincingly, "This color just makes the room look so ... so ... warm!"

I'll remind her of the dangers of renovation: "Remember when I painted the living room and climbed up on the mantelpiece and it fell off the wall?" (True story, as well as the reason our mantel clock always reads "2:36" and none of the family photos have glass anymore.)

Sometimes, I just fall back on a lame "You know, I really like this place now that we've finished everything!" As the party got closer, I thought I was in the clear.

Then, the other night, my wife called me into the dining room. I saw to my horror that she had color cards in her hand.

"I've never liked this wallpaper," she said, shaking her head, "Don't you think it's a little ... dark?" My only feeling for the red flowered wallpaper was the grating memory of putting it up five years ago, late into the night, before the twins' christening party.

"Why do you ask?" I said innocently.

"The seams are curling up," she said, "And this red is a very harsh color!"

"Can't we just get some super glue and maybe turn down the lights a little?" (I know, it wasn't convincing even when I said it.)

As she started trying to find a shade that would pick up the colors in the drapes, I put my foot down.

"I am not going to spend the whole week before the party painting the dining room!" I bellowed, in that tone that says I mean business. (I am beginning to believe I need to get a new tone, as this one clearly doesn't work.)

"I don't expect you to spend the whole week on this," she said. "You'll need to get this finished up quickly if we want to get the hallway done by Saturday."

I turned and noticed that she had taped up color cards to the wall in the front hall. I held up my hand. "Not gonna happen!" I said. I marched off to bed, cutting off all further talk on the subject.

The next day, I came home from work and walked into the dining room. All of my kids were on chairs, stepladders and, in one case, balanced on a sideboard, busily pulling my red flowered wallpaper off the walls. Try to get them to do something constructive, such as cleaning their rooms, and watch 'em scatter. But destructive projects will draw them like flies.

There were soggy lumps of wallpaper everywhere, with more coming down in great damp sheets. My 8-year-old son was in charge of the spray bottle, soaking the walls, the woodwork and, of course, his sisters.

"Hey, Daddy, Daddy!" one of the twins called out. "Surprised?"

"No," I said, tossing my briefcase into a corner. "Not particularly." I loosened my tie and went up to change into my painting clothes.

The Unkindest Cut

With school coming around, it was time this weekend for my boys' end-of-summer trim.

I usually give them one good shearing at the beginning of the summer, and then another in mid-July, when they grow out and begin to resemble bad toupees. But I also make sure that they start the school year with a neat haircut. I do this myself not because of tradition, or because I am a talented hair stylist, or even because I think of myself as the king of D-I-Y, but because I am cheap.

A haircut these days, even at a discount chain, runs about $14. And while I realize that a professional job would look neater and more attractive, I also take into account that my boys aren't sticklers for appearances. (My youngest once wore the same T-shirt five days in a row, taking it off at night to "air out." Another boy walked around for a week with a melted caramel in his hair, not even curious as to what it might be.) Opting for a store-bought trim job then, seems like throwing money away.

I have experimented with all types of styles, but settled on one basic cut: crew cut length on the sides, 3/4 inch on top. It's not the most stylish look, but it's fast, sort of like shearing sheep. It also has the advantage that little can go wrong. Nothing sticks out funny or looks choppy when it's all one length, and there's no "blending" required. (My 8-year-old pleaded this year for a "Ranger Cut," something he had seen in a war movie. He asked me to shave his head, except for the very top, which should have a small circle of hair. I refused, telling him that what looks tough on a trooper might make a kid his age just look inbred.)

The boys really don't like to have me do their hair. I have more than once drawn blood as I attempted to work my way around their ears. But they can be bribed into it. I've put out a standing offer that I would split the savings accrued by forgoing the barbershop. They walk away from the whole experience a little misshapen and with a minor laceration or two, but $7 richer. My oldest son opted out of this whole system a couple of years ago. When I tried to get him back in the fold, offering him the whole $14, he told me, "Dad, you pay me once for the haircut. I pay at school for weeks!"

My mother, probably for the same reasons that got me started, used to cut our hair when my brothers and I were growing up. She did not like us to go off to school with perfectly straight bangs, as the neighbor kids used to call out "Hey Moe, where's Larry and Curly?" And styling gel had not yet been invented, or at least it was not used on males of the species who wanted to survive the playground.

So she invented her own style. Our bangs were cut at a 30-degree angle, giving the impression, at least from a distance, that we had combed our hair to the side. Our friends and neighbors got used to our lopsided look, and rarely commented on it, but strangers would often stare for a moment, and our annual school pictures looked right only if tilted at a slight angle.

I do feel a little guilty about convincing our boys to forgo proper haircuts, especially as the clippers I have used for the past 10 years are not technically for human use. (The drugstore where I shopped had sold out of haircutting kits, but the clerk whispered to me that I could buy the exact same hair trimmer in the Pet Grooming section one aisle over, and would save $3. I also got a coupon for dog biscuits.)

And the mess left drives my wife insane. I usually set up shop in the master bathroom over the sink. I try my best to clean up the piles of clippings but usually miss a hair or two. (My wife angrily points this out to me as she is brushing her teeth with a woolly toothbrush or trying to insert a furry contact lens.)

Still, I felt a certain sense of pride and satisfaction as each of my younger boys left the bathroom this weekend with a semi-professional cut and $7 in his pocket. I even got a little choked up as I called out, "Make sure you get a bandage on that before you go outside!"

The Deep Freeze

When we got a large secondhand freezer for our basement, we thought, as most people do, that it would simplify our lives.

We'd have Tupperware ready after each meal, and leftovers would be carefully labeled and stored away for later enjoyment. Shopping trips would be more economical, as we'd be able to take advantage of BOGOs (Buy One, Get One). And best of all, we'd be able to clear a little room in our kitchen freezer, which had grown so crowded we could no longer see what was in it, let alone eat any of it. Every time I opened the door, an ice cream carton would fall out and hit me on the toe.

But reality was a little disappointing. First, while we have at least 47 plastic containers, not one of them has a lid that fits. And what food we did store away just didn't seem worth thawing months later, when it might be spaghetti sauce, or maybe chili, but is probably just taco sauce.

On a typical day, our basement freezer contains a variety of items that are for various reasons inedible. There are two or three loaves of frost-encrusted bread. You can always find the lumpy remnants of someone's ice-cream birthday cake, a little hard on top. It's next to three or four paint rollers and brushes (it's easier than cleaning them) and an assortment of chicken parts that once were quite fresh, but now, after some unknown period, are about as appetizing as that Stone-Age guy found frozen in the Alps a few years ago.

There is also one 23 1/2-inch brown trout I caught five years ago. (I know that this is supposed to be about my freezer, but it really was an incredible fish. I have been waiting two years to brag about it in a column.)

The problem is caused by our kids, who seem to know how to get the freezer open (it has a lock) but not how to shut it. The effects are nasty: Ice cream becomes rubbery, Popsicles are misshapen, and hamburgers take on a blue-gray tinge. This constant freeze-thaw cycle has also created a monster frost buildup inside the door that begins to encase everything in its path with ice. After a few weeks, it looks as if it could take on the Titanic.

The worst incident was this past fall when my eldest son decided to preserve his Halloween candy in the freezer. As a teenager, he was probably too old to trick or treat, but he and a few friends decided to make one last run at it, and each collected a year's supply of candy. He came in the door with an old pillowcase filled with about 40 pounds of chocolate bars, which he inventoried and then stowed in the freezer.

All was fine until the other kids' Halloween candy ran out a few weeks later. As my eldest continued to publicly chow down on Snickers and Hershey bars well after the traditional feasting period, the younger ones got suspicious. They began following him around and whispering about the location of his secret "stash." One of the twins was assigned to innocently ask for a piece of candy while the other tailed him.

His fatal mistake was allowing his 8-year-old brother to see him coming out of the basement with a box of frosty Junior Mints. Within hours, the word had spread, and soon, the other children were slipping into the basement with shifty looks. The signs of secretive gorging were everywhere: kids walking around with cocoa smiles, no one hungry at dinner and wrappers found under beds, tucked in side-table drawers and down the cushions of the couch.

Then one day, we went down to the basement to find a debacle. One candy thief had left the freezer door open - way open - and the basement floor was a small sea of melted iceberg, soggy candy wrappers, half-thawed half-freezer-burned burgers, rotting chicken legs and one pretty ripe 23 1/2-inch trout. To make matters worse, the freezer itself was shuddering and shooting off sparks as the melting ice ran into the electric motor at the bottom.

I acted quickly. I ran back to the basement steps and began shouting at the top of my lungs that whoever had left the freezer door open had better start throwing his or her clothes into a backpack, as it was "Orphanage Time."

It took me an hour to find the culprit, two hours to clean out the freezer, and three days to calm down. Everything, and I mean everything, had to be thrown out.

Except my trout. To be safe, I now keep it in the kitchen freezer.

Cold Feet

I am the proud owner of more than 40 pairs of socks. Some are black, some white, and at least three or four have some sort of argyle design.

I am not sure of the exact descriptions or numbers, as I have not seen most of these socks in ages. I buy them, wear them once and put them down the laundry chute with the other dirty clothes. As the socks disappear into the darkness, I silently bid them goodbye. I almost certainly will never see them again, at least not in matched pairs.

Like many modern couples, my wife and I split up the household chores. On nights when she cooks (most nights), I do the dishes. On those few occasions when I cook, she is in charge of scraping all the food the kids won't eat into the trash and pouring them bowls of cereal after I have left the room.

Some chores, though, are firmly in one corner or the other. For instance, I am completely responsible for cutting the grass, putting up storm windows and killing spiders. My wife does all the laundry. And for the most part, it gets done. There are few instances where someone has had to wear dirty clothes to school. But she cannot, no matter how hard she tries (or, for that matter, how hard I whine) bring herself to fold and put away socks.

My wife's problem with socks goes beyond the norm. Like many families, we have a sock basket where all the mismatched socks go after each load of laundry. But in our case, every sock goes into the basket -- even those socks that are clearly right next to their mates. Folding socks is a tedious job and therefore best taken care of tomorrow. But tomorrow, at least for our socks, never comes.

At some point, the basket of socks gets too full, or company knocks unexpectedly at the door, and my wife gets panicky and hides the basket someplace out of sight. I have found sock baskets in the spare room, in the basement and once, in the bottom of the grandfather clock. In cleaning out a little-used closet last month, I found a bunch of socks from the early '90s. Some were baby socks belonging to a child who now stands 5 feet 2 inches.

My wife has come up with her own solution to this problem: She has decided to go sockless all year. She claims it is a fashion statement and that wearing socks makes her uncomfortable. I know better. It's the matching and folding of socks that she can't deal with.

No matter how much I complain, my wife comes up with a response. The first line of defense is a blank stare. Although it has come up dozens, maybe hundreds, of times, this whole problem is new to her. Then she looks indignant and claims that she just put a big pile of socks on my dresser a couple days ago. When that fails, (all I have to do is open my sock drawer, which contains nothing but a few dimes) she says that I must be overreacting, as there are tons of socks in her drawer. I point out that she wears only two or three pairs per year, which makes it tough to run out.

Finally, she calmly and coldly presses the nuclear button, saying the one thing she knows will make me back down, the one thing that will shut me up.

"If it's that bad," she says indignantly, "you can start doing the laundry yourself!"

One morning, after hunting for a pair of clean black socks for 15 minutes, I sat down and ran the numbers. Fifteen minutes each morning totals up to almost 91 hours each year just spent looking for socks. I stormed down the stairs.

"This is ridiculous!" I shouted. "I ought to just buy a can of black paint and dip my feet in each morning so I don't have to go through this every day!" The point was, of course, to show how desperate the situation had become, how enraged I was.

My wife just looked at me, blinked once, and said, "Now, that's a solution."

She smiled and went upstairs, her bare feet padding softly on the carpet.

Beware of Wives Bearing Funeral Arrangements

It has probably been going on for quite a while, but I have only noticed it during the past few years. My wife, like many people, has become obsessed with death. The problem is that she doesn't think about the subject in a general way, or even about her own death. She seems to spend a good deal of time and energy ruminating on the circumstances of my death.

I first noticed this one afternoon when we were discussing funeral options. I mentioned that I did not particularly look forward to the idea of being buried. I have decayed so rapidly as it is. I felt that once I had stopped breathing, it was probably too late to begin working on preservation. I said that, instead, I'd like to be cremated and have my ashes tossed from my favorite rock on the river upstate, where I like to fish.

My wife, who had been listening only halfheartedly, suddenly took a real interest in the subject and began throwing out suggestions. We could have a little ceremony on the riverbank, she said, and she knew of a stone carver who could probably engrave a touching comment into the side of the rock so that it would be more meaningful.

Very sweet, but I couldn't help but be taken aback with the enthusiasm with which she was sketching all this out. With the same wistful looks that some women get when looking forward to their daughter's wedding, my wife was picking out music for the moment my earthly remains were "scattered" in the current and wondering aloud whether you needed a permit for such a thing.

From then on, I began to notice that she inserted the phrase "If something were to happen to you ..." into a lot of our conversations. Usually it was followed by a phrase such as "I'd stay single unless I met someone who could be patient with the kids" or "I think I'd keep the house, but I imagine the mortgage payments might be tough."

When she gets aggravated at me, it's often followed by "I'm going to bury you in your pajamas in a cardboard box and take a cruise with the funeral money!" She noticed in an offhand way that the UPS man would make a great "second" husband. When I got night sweats last year, I found that my wife had printed out page after page of Web sites diagnosing possible "conditions." Most gave me from six months to a year to live.

It's not just my wife anymore either. I had to climb to the top of our slate roof last month to clear a small tree growing in one of our gutters. In the past, she had been worried sick when I took on such dangerous jobs. This time she only asked how much life insurance I carried.

When I reached the roof, it was worse.

Stretching out with a broom handle while holding onto the side of our chimney, I tried to dislodge the offending seedling. Then I noticed my wife and twin daughters in the back yard. They had set up three lawn chairs in a row and were sitting as if at a movie. They wanted good seats, they said, so they wouldn't miss anything. I looked down from my precarious situation, wondering if they were planning a shopping trip to pick out three tasteful (but cute) black dresses.

To be fair, this particular trait does run in my wife's family. My mother-in-law last year made her husband clean out his old clothes from his closet because, she said, she didn't want to have to do it "later." But the idea that this matter-of-fact approach would be passed on to another generation, and that my daughters might end up as eager little grim reapers to their husbands, makes me nervous.

Earlier this week, I was washing my sports car in the driveway. It's not that great a car (it has no first gear, the windows leak, and it won't start when the temperature drops below 52 degrees) but it's fast and red, and when it does start, it makes me feel more like a kid than a cadaver. My 6-year-old daughter came out on the back porch and watched me for a few minutes.

"I like your sports car," Olivia said sweetly.

"Thanks, honey," I said, smiling and waving at her.

"I hope I get it when you're dead!" she said, then winked at me and walked off.

Driven To Distraction

This past month, my wife and I had to come to grips with a horror that tests the resolve of every family: My eldest son got his learner's permit.

My main worry is that with his genetic legacy, my son would have no natural talent for operating a motor vehicle. My wife has, in the years since we met in college, rear-ended another car, clipped off the end of our picket fence and burned up the engine in her sister's Dodge Dart when she drove 90 miles after the "oil" light came on. Once, in a masterstroke, she got our car stuck in a drive-through car wash.

As a teen-ager, I seriously damaged the transmission of my father's car when I hit a boulder while driving across a field to impress my friends. I didn't mention it to my father at the time and most certainly didn't bring it up a week later when the transmission fell off as my father drove us through the steaming Everglades on a trip in Florida. (I knew my father too well for that -- too many swamps and hungry alligators around for a confession.) As a matter of fact, I never got around to telling him about the transmission, as I could never come up with a good explanation as to why I had his car in the field in the first place.

My experience in learning to drive was traumatic. I started out with my father in the deserted parking lot of a local shopping mall at 6 a.m. one Sunday. My father figured it best to try this out in an area where there was little chance of killing anyone but ourselves.

The problem, of course, is that the lanes were only 100 yards long and that there were no traffic signs. My father dealt with this by shouting out "Stop sign!" or "Yield!" to simulate being faced with sudden decisions. He would also bark out things like "Dog!" or "Old woman!" That first lesson lasted approximately 11 1/2 minutes. I had missed a "stop sign" and had run over a make-believe child and his invisible dog.

My wife took my son on one of his first driving forays. I was not along. (For safety's sake, one of us always remains behind to raise the children.) While it was only to the supermarket and back, my impression was that it did not go well. My son came home, angrily tossed the keys on the counter and stomped off to his room. My wife stumbled in, looking as if she'd seen a ghost.

"Did he complain that I screamed?" she said indignantly. "I'm sorry, but people do that when they're about to die."

After that, driving lessons were up to me.

Remembering my short, tense drive with my dad, I wanted to make sure that this was a bonding experience. My son's 16th birthday came right at the time we were spending a weekend in the country. This gave us a chance to hone his skills in a sparsely populated area, where the property damages might be lower.

We started out on a country road, my son sitting nervously behind the wheel and me in the passenger seat, suddenly wondering whether our car was equipped with passenger-side air bags. My son started out on the road cautiously, wanting to make sure that he got a feel for the engine on our big SUV.

"You can probably speed up a little," I said, "the speed limit is 35."

"How fast am I going?" he asked, not wanting to take his eyes off the road.

I glanced over at the speedometer. "Nine miles per hour." I checked the mirror for angry tailgaters.

Suddenly, the car shot forward and I realized how astronauts feel when the main booster kicks in. As we reached a long downhill stretch, I tried to muster the control to keep from screaming myself. "Not ... that ... fast!" I said through clenched teeth.

"You said to go faster!" he complained, still unable to look at the speedometer as it inched higher.

Bracing my feet on the windshield, I closed my eyes. "Stop sign!" I called out. "Child! Old woman! Invisible dog!"

My son slowed the car and pulled over onto the gravel berm. He stared at me for a moment, shook his head, then pulled out again, this time at a more reasonable pace, no doubt vowing to do a better job with his son.

My Old Swing Set Injury

This week, one of our twin 6-year-old girls came down with a bad cough. She tumbled out of bed, pulled on her oversized robe and shuffled into the kitchen looking like a miniature zombie. While she didn't have a temperature, her cough made her sound like a sea lion with chronic asthma. We steered her to the living room couch, wrapped her in a blanket and put on cartoons. Then, we called the school to say that she'd be missing in action for the day.

Within minutes, her twin sister and her 8-year-old brother magically came down with the same symptoms. As I tried to wrestle them into their jackets and backpacks, they held their heads and stomachs (covering both bases), and moaned that they were ailing, too. In an Oscar-worthy performance, my son made choking sounds and opened his mouth, fishlike, as if he were going to bring up his Honey-Nut Cheerios. I got a small lump in my throat as I opened the front door and shoved the little brats out with the sole of my shoe.

I shouldn't be that surprised, as I am sure they inherited the "faker" gene from me. I was, in my time, the ninja master of faux illnesses.

When I was about 7, I was climbing on top of a swing set at a neighbor's house, and I slipped off. I fell directly across one of the wooden swings below, taking a hard blow to the stomach. I then flipped over and landed in the dust flat on my back. The adults who were there rushed to my aid, thinking that I was dead (the parents who owned the swing set no doubt were more concerned at the thought of getting sued by my parents).

While I was fine, I did have a sore stomach that kept me in bed for the next couple of days. (Actually, the stomach kept me in bed for about six hours. After that, it was the lure of 'round-the-clock attention and endless "Brady Bunch" reruns that held me in place.) And while the pain went away rather quickly, my efforts to milk the incident for attention lasted for months. Any morning when I didn't feel like going to school, I'd get out of bed, adopt the appropriate pained look and then crawl downstairs holding my stomach.

"My old swing-set injury ... " I'd gasp. Then, I'd lean against the kitchen table, one hand on my stomach, the other wiping sweat from my brow. The second best thing about this was when mother led me to the couch, where I could lie under a blanket and watch game shows and reruns until afternoon cartoons came on. (In my day, there was no such thing as Nickelodeon or the Cartoon Network. With cartoons 24/7, it is a wonder kids leave the couch at all these days.)

The absolute first best thing about those mornings, though, was watching my older brother seethe at my getting away with this for maybe the 20th time. "Mom!" he'd scream at the top of his lungs. "He's faking it!" I would watch as he had to be literally forced out the door, protesting the whole way. Then, I would run to the window, wait to catch his eye and then smile like a nasty Cheshire cat as he stomped off toward school.

Falling off the swing set was one of the smartest things I did as a kid. A couple of hours of pain paid off in at least 20 to 30 days of school-free living, the TV watching interrupted only by my occasional calls for more chocolate milk.

After I had taken my two healthy but miserably unhappy kids to the bus, and waved goodbye to their glum faces through the bus windows, I walked back to our house. I stood outside the living room window long enough to see my daughter, standing on the coffee table, dancing up a storm to some song on TV.

I went to the front stoop, fumbled loudly with the knob and then threw open the door, just in time to catch my daughter sliding back under her covers, a sad and sickly look on her face. I walked over and leaned down to feel her forehead.

"You OK?" I asked. She nodded, sticking out her lower lip.

"I'll be upstairs," I told her. "Remember, don't start dancing again until I get out of the room." Her eyes popped open.

As I walked up the stairs, I smiled, knowing that the master had successfully passed on his skills to a new generation.

The Sweat Shop

This past week, a sudden heat wave brought on one of the most hated rituals of old-house living, the annual lugging of air conditioners up from the basement. I try to put off getting out the air conditioners as long as possible. They don't usually go in until we have experienced at least three or four steamy nights in a row, and until my wife has issued her third or fourth ultimatum. And each fall, I delay in removing them again until they are covered with an inch of snow. Putting it off like this is particularly stupid, as it allows me to experience both the sleepless nights and the pain and suffering of lugging the conditioners up the steps.

This year, I had expected to hold off a few more days, but when I got home from work on Monday, I found the entire crew in a particularly steamy (and grumpy) mood. They were all draped across the furniture like wet rags, fanning themselves. The twins, covered with sweat, were even too tired to squabble with each other. Most hot days, the kids cool off at the community pool. This day, however, the pool visit had been cut short when some joker tossed a Snickers bar into the pool. As a precaution, and in case it only "looked" like a Snickers, the pool had been shut down for an extended period of sanitation, and the kids had to come home.

I tried to make light of it, telling them that I had been perfectly comfortable in my air-conditioned office, but that only seemed to make things worse. So I was forced to make my way into the darkest corner of the basement, clear away cobwebs and Halloween decorations, and stumble up the steps with the air conditioners.

I use the term "air conditioners" here very loosely. Most of our units have been donated (meaning dumped) by well-meaning neighbors who have installed central air and no longer needed the window units. They take pity on us, knowing that we will probably remain, Amish-like, without the comforts of modern life. Over the years, our house has become a retirement home for old air conditioners, a place where they can rest after a hard life, where they won't do much except sit around, and where they can die in peace.

There are five air conditioners in our basement. Three work well enough to cool a small room (up to coat closet size). One blows only slightly cool air. The fifth, in some bit of sick, twisted irony, actually blows hot air. What they all have in common, however, is weight. Each is around 2,000 pounds and comes equipped with razor-like fins on the back. These fins, it seems, are necessary for air cooling, but as our air conditioners no longer function all that well, the little fins seem only to serve as a way for me to donate blood twice a year.

The air conditioner I hate the most is in our garage. It was brought over in a wheelbarrow one steamy day by a sympathetic neighbor with the warning that he wasn't sure if it worked. After this description, I tried to block his way by lying across our driveway. My wife, however, took a practical approach and told him to put it in our garage, as we could always get it fixed. (In my experience, I have never seen anyone get an air conditioner fixed. The common practice is to go out and buy a new one, then dump the old one at my house.)

Six years later, it sits in the same corner, looking filthy, taking up space and getting in the way. (When I complain, my wife tells me that the same description could, theoretically, fit me.)

We have investigated the idea of getting central air installed but rejected it. Our house is heated by radiators rather than forced air. It would mean installing vents, which in turn would mean ripping out half our walls. It has taken me almost 10 years to get our house painted and papered the way we like it, and it would take another 10, I'm sure, to clean up after all that renovation work. So I continue, year after year, like some sad, suburban Sisyphus, to carry my air conditioners up and down the basement stairs.

If it hadn't been for that clown with the Snickers bar, I'd have been able to hold out for three more weeks.

Waste Not, Want Not

When I was a little kid, one of the worst things you could be called was "trash picker." The idea, of course, was that you came from such poverty that you got clothes or toys only by raiding the neighbors' refuse. But my wife and I have, over the years, done quite nicely by doing just that.

We don't roam the streets of our neighborhood before dawn, pulling apart Hefty bags and emptying them on the curb. But if we are driving along and see some abandoned treasure sitting out for the trash, we may launch an impromptu rescue operation. One of us (usually my wife) will be the lookout, while the other (usually, and reluctantly, I) will be in charge of slipping out of the car and grabbing the prize. Over the years, we have snagged an old school desk, a wooden bench, assorted lamps and, once, a color TV.

Before anyone gets too indignant, I can assure you we're not the only ones who make a habit out of rummaging through others' rubbish. It is the secret vice of the suburbs. One of our neighbors picked up a screen door that fit his house perfectly, and another couple we know used a "found" dresser as the base for their powder-room sink. Friends of ours in Virginia picked up some toddler toys from their next-door neighbor's trash. Every time the previous owners came by to visit, our friends would have to hide the toys in a cupboard.

Early in our marriage, we lived in a town house in a Washington suburb, with barely enough money to keep the lights on, let alone buy furnishings. Late one evening, we found a nice cream-colored rug in a nearby town after visiting friends for dinner. The rug was neatly rolled up in front of a stately house. (We have our standards -- we pick trash only from the best houses.)

We drove by three times, sizing up our prey before we struck. My wife jumped behind the wheel of the car, and I threw the rug into the trunk. At 12 by 17 feet, it fit nicely in a basement room we were remodeling, and the huge stains we found when we unrolled it (spilled chocolate milk, we told each other, trying not to think of the alternatives) corresponded almost exactly with the placement of our furniture, so it didn't look that bad, either.

A year later, when we put the town house on the market, the buyer (for some reason) made it a condition of the sale that we leave that carpet in the basement. I can only imagine the screams of terror when his wife walked in after closing and saw the room without the conveniently placed furniture.

This nefarious activity has continued almost everywhere we've lived (except, of course, in New York City, where a rolled-up carpet might contain a neighbor's wife). Not everyone in our family is thrilled with our collection of "found" items. My 13-year-old son refuses to sit on used furniture, citing the real but unlikely prospect that it might have been, in his words, "puked on or something worse." (I have tried but cannot envision what something "worse" than that could be.)

Last month, I was cleaning out our garage and found two little play kitchenettes our twin girls had used when they were younger. A couple of years ago, I stowed them in the back of the garage and then never got them out again. They were now filthy, and one seemed to have spent some time as a hideout for stray cats. I grabbed one and walked it down to the curb, then went back to get the other kitchenette. As I walked back, I came across a young mother pushing a stroller with a 1-year-old girl. A second daughter, probably 3, stood by anxiously. The mother had snagged the first kitchenette and was trying to balance it on the stroller and make a quick getaway.

As I came down the driveway, she looked up in embarrassment. "I'm so sorry," she said. "Are these yours?"

I smiled and told her she was welcome to take it, as well as the one I had in my hands.

"I'm so embarrassed," she said. "I didn't know you were home."

"That's OK," I assured her. "Our girls have outgrown them."

As I walked up the driveway, I fondly remembered the day my wife had picked out those little kitchenettes. I sat by with the motor running, keeping a lookout for anyone we knew.

TV in Hell

For the past few weeks, we have been able to experience what TV must be like in hell.

I am not referring to any particular programming, not even to the thankfully departed sitcom "Emiril." I am talking instead about the color on our set.

One evening last month, as we were watching "Friends," the screen suddenly blinked, and when it came back, it had changed from full color to an odd red tinge. It was as if all other colors had been wiped out of the universe, leaving only red, light red and dark red.

I sat forward, squinting at the set, and told the kids that there was something wrong with our cable. One of the children sighed and informed me that it had been happening for weeks. No one had told me, it turned out, because they were afraid I would start tinkering with the set again, turning it for all intents and purposes into a radio.

The TV has been an issue in our house for years, as it continues to take on new ailments. The sound cuts in and out, the picture is unreliable and when you press the volume control, the channel changes. While it has served faithfully for years, it has now reached the point where if it were a major league pitcher, it would be patted on the back and pulled from the game. Were it a race horse, it would now be soap.

At first, watching our favorite TV shows in variations of red was disconcerting. It looked as if "ER" was a medical show set in a darkroom or the control room of a sub. Everyone on TV was now a redhead. True redheads, like Carrot Top, now looked like their heads were on fire. Dramas took on an evil glow, and comedies seemed somehow depressing.

This did, however, give me a chance to teach the younger kids about colors. I was able to explain that all the colors in the world could be made up from just three primary colors: red, blue and yellow. When mixed together at different levels, anything was possible. Our set, I explained, was now missing the blue and yellow colors, and that was why everything seemed so off. The children, however, had follow-up questions, as they always do.

"Why don't you just refill the blue and yellow cartridges?" one asked, believing that televisions were like ink jet printers. I tried to explain that televisions were so complicated, and circuits so tiny, that no human alive could fix them, and that should anything go wrong, there was no alternative but putting them out on the curb for the trash men.

"Is it still called 'Blue's Clues' if he isn't blue anymore?" queried another. I assured her that it would not matter. She agreed, telling me that her kindergarten teacher had taught them that you could be anything you wanted, and that a person's color did not make any difference.

One of the older boys got to the real point. "How come you're so cheap that you don't just go out and get a new set?" he asked. "They're not that expensive!"

I was about to explain that "expensive" was a relative term, and that money didn't grow on trees, blah, blah blah... (I would not have really said "blah, blah blah." I would have continued with a litany of remarks designed to make him feel guilty for being so materialistic and insensitive for calling me cheap. But since he would not have listened to a word of it, I don't believe it's worth forcing on readers, either. Besides, he probably has a point about being cheap.)

For the time being, we content ourselves with our red-soaked television experience. We are now used to it. It only comes up at odd times, when my teenager has a friend over and I hear the inevitable, "Dude, your set is whacked. Let's go to my house." (This of course, has the advantage of clearing my house of teenagers, and could lead to a whole new industry.)

Every once in a while, however, the set will blink again, and for a few minutes, full color will come back on. It is disconcerting. The colors are too bright, too garish. We feel like coal miners coming out after a day's labor, waiting for our eyes to adjust. But before that can happen, the set usually blinks again, and we are thrown back into our comfortable crimson world, where every actor has a sunburn, every scene seems to take place on Mars and Carrot Top's head is on always on fire.

The Coffee Clutch

I grew up drinking coffee. Like my eight brothers and sisters, I started around age 12, working my way up from a half cup with lots of milk to an adult mug of strong java.

As kids, we were encouraged by our parents to drink coffee as soon as we were able to stand it. (Considering how many children my mother produced, I often wonder if she was really trying to stunt our growth, and keep us from growing out of our clothes.) With all those kids slumped around the kitchen table (half of them smoking cigarettes), our kitchen looked more like a junior truck stop than the Waltons' home. We often went through two pots in a morning.

As a young boy, I had the daily chore of preparing the coffee for the next morning. We had a huge 25-cup barrel-shaped tin coffee pot, the kind found today only in church basements. Where modern coffee makers are made of glass and plastic, ours was about the shape and size of R2D2, and was fairly heavy when full. My coffee was occasionally the source of complaints. (I knew you had to change the water each day but was under the impression the grounds could be reused.) But no one refused to drink it.

As an adult, I have continued to enjoy a cup of coffee in the morning. I usually drank whatever brand happened to be on sale and frankly couldn't tell the difference between a full-bodied Arabica and Sanka. While most of the country has been lining up at Starbucks, ordering half latte dark roast espresso mochalinos, I have been on the sidelines, too confused to even try to place an order.

I had a wake-up call, however, when we visited friends this spring. Having traveled regularly to Italy, these friends are a bit more sophisticated than we are. (Nothing to brag about, as I believe that there are people in the hills of Appalachia, married to siblings, who are more sophisticated than we are.) Our friends had developed a taste for good wines -- and morning doses of cappuccino.

When they first offered us a cup, I was wary, but I felt comfortable among friends and agreed. The coffee came in a little can imported from Italy, and the grounds were black as tar. The coffee was strong enough to loosen the fillings in my molars, and the accompanying caffeine rush was so powerful that I felt as if I had two paddles pressed to my chest. I could almost hear the attending physician call out, "Clear!"

From the first sip, however, my wife was hooked. When we got home, she ordered me to go out and buy our own cappuccino maker. I generally avoid appliances that build up great pressure and steam under the theory that I want to avoid being punctured and scalded in my kitchen. But I gave in. I bought the cheapest machine they sold, thinking that if it broke quickly, my wife's obsession with high-octane coffee might end as well.

The first few mornings, we each had just one syrupy cup. At my wife's urging, we soon moved up to two. One morning, as we finished our second, my wife looked across the table at me. "How 'bout just one more cup?" she asked.

I shrugged in agreement, thinking that it couldn't hurt. If two cups woke me up with a jolt, three might make me alert enough to actually accomplish something. But I reached my limit after just the first few sips. My head began to buzz, I felt my heartbeat getting a little erratic, and my frazzled synapses produced a wavy apparition of Juan Valdez and his donkey standing in the corner.

My wife, however, had developed a serious coffee jones, and couldn't stop. Where she used to sip slowly, she now gulped and sometimes finished her cup before I'd had a chance to sit down with mine. Our house began to smell like the Chock Full O' Nuts factory.

It came to a head one morning when my wife eagerly suggested a fourth cup. I finally put my foot down. "That's it!" I said. "I think you have a problem!"

"Just one more?" she asked, holding her cup out like a shaky, French-roasted Oliver Twist.

I nodded slowly, afraid to confront her in this state. I made her another cup -- then pulled out the phone book to see if there was a listing for Javaholics Anonymous.

Great Balls of Fire

Each year, as the weather gets warmer and the sun stays around a little later, I get excited about grilling again. While I stick mostly to chicken and burgers (an experiment with spare ribs three years ago resulted in a ball of flame that could be seen by astronauts in the space shuttle), I think I have become a master of the basics.

My art suffers, however, because of my shoddy instrument. I am like a virtuoso playing on a plastic violin, a Winslow Homer forced to use poster paints.

The only grill I can afford is a bottom-of-the-line job at the home center, the $109 special that takes three hours to bolt together and then leans precariously on spindly legs. It starts rusting almost before the assembly process is finished, and its grates warp within weeks. It's as if all the other guys in the neighborhood drive Cadillacs, and I'm stuck on a moped.

I dream of a Weber or an Aussie, maybe even a Jenn-Air -- a grill with finely tuned burners, one that could hold the heat properly, distribute it evenly and, above all, make me look cool. What a master chef like me really deserves is a big heavy unit with a cast-iron grate and distributor. What I end up with is a grill that lasts through one summer and, when uncovered the next spring, is little more than the decaying corpse of last year's grill.

That's why I came up with my scheme. I found a big barrel-shaped charcoal grill at the home center that had all the features I was looking for: the cast-iron grilling surface, the solid construction and the big professional look. It even had a smokestack with a little flapper at the top.

I started brainstorming, drawing a little diagram on the back of a sale flier. Using a replacement cast-iron distributor and the valves and hoses from our old grill, and by drilling a few holes in the body, I could convert it to a gas grill and create the equivalent of a $600 grill for about $135. I pulled aside one of the clerks in the home center and showed him my diagram.

"Ever heard of anyone doing that?" I asked.

He stared at me with a mix of pity and annoyance. "No." he said. "Never. Most of our customers, far as I can tell, don't want to die."

Someone, it seems, had forgotten the cardinal rule about the customer always being right. I went home and dashed off a quick e-mail to the charcoal grill company. After lavishly praising its grill, I described my plan in detail and asked whether it had been done before. Within an hour I got back a terse message from the company's legal department, stating that, for liability reasons, it could not condone such an action. I alone would be responsible for the consequences.

My wife was, sadly enough, not surprised to hear of my plans. She has seen more than her fill of my whacked-out money-saving ideas. (It was OK when I used an old eight-track stereo to give our TV a theater sound system, but she drew the line when our first son was born and I showed her my technical drawings for a money-saving breast pump that involved the vacuum cleaner.)

This time she simply smiled over her newspaper and said, "Go for it, Tiger." (She never actually calls me Tiger, and this alone should cause suspicion.)

"Really?" I said.

"No, not really!" she said. "I can't believe I married you."

At this point, I got indignant. "Hey, I even ran it by the people at the grill company. They didn't rule it out. Not completely."

She walked away with her usual response in such situations: "You kill yourself doing this, and I won't even bury you. I'll leave you out there and let raccoons eat you."

I haven't given up. I still intend to carry out my plan, but I will do more research. Sometime in the next month, slow down as you pass my house. You will see a proud chef triumphantly grilling on a solid piece of equipment worthy of his culinary skills.

If, however, you see a guy running around in circles covered in flames, please stop and squirt the hose for a few minutes and help me into the house.

If not, the raccoons might get me.

Gas Pains

My plan to buy a charcoal smoker and convert it to a gas grill did not come without risk. On one hand, I'd get a great grill at a fraction of the cost of a Jenn-Air. On the other, I might end up as a suburban legend: the man who played with fire and ended up blasting over the horizon, leaving behind a trail of purple smoke and charred docksiders on the patio.

The entire setup process was made a little bit harder by my cheering section -- my wife and oldest son sitting in lawn chairs, drinking sodas and reading the paper, looking up every three or four minutes to make sarcastic comments about my ability to survive this project. My wife pretended to call and increase my life insurance while my son asked if he could have my car. (I vowed to myself that if I were to erupt in flames, I'd take at least one of them with me.)

Once the charcoal grill was assembled, the fun part began. I had to drill holes in the front, hack apart the inner workings and make way for the gas assembly. It is not often in life that one gets the chance to buy something new, take it home and assemble it, then start attacking it with power tools. I had a fancy gold diamond-encrusted drill bit I bought last winter that the manufacturer claims can cut through anything on earth. I paid $8 for it, picturing all the things I might want to perforate, and then never used it. This was my chance.

The drill bit worked as advertised, and metal shavings flew right and left as I blew new holes into the front of the grill. (Just two of the holes were necessary to let the gas lines in. I drilled the other ones just because I got carried away.) Then I attacked our old gas grill, cutting off the valves and controls so I could use them on the new grill.

As I stood over the grill and dropped in a match, I said a silent prayer. This would either be my moment of triumph or the moment I'd be sent into the skies like an oversized bottle rocket.

I turned the dials and grinned as the grill lit up with even blue flames. It worked perfectly. I closed the lid and sat back with a beer to watch the built-in thermometer rise. Slowly but surely, the dial moved ...

It started at 75 degrees, then slowly made its way up: 85 degrees ... 95 degrees ...

I felt like Dr. Frankenstein waiting for my monster to come alive. 105 degrees, 115 degrees ...

I played with the little hatch on the smokestack, feeling the heated air flowing out, and dreamed of my new career: "Peter McKay started out with a great idea, retrofitting charcoal grills with gas, and built it into a small empire. Today, the 'Grill King' turns out 10,000 units per day."

Lost in my reverie, I forgot to watch the thermometer -- 165 degrees and steady. I checked the tank to make sure it was full and checked the valves to make sure that they were open all the way. Looking inside, I saw the little blue flames still popping away. I closed the lid again and tapped the dial. Steady at 165.

This couldn't be. While not exactly comfortable, 165 degrees isn't hot enough to cook anything. Hamburgers would be finished faster if I just put them on the front seat of the car, rolled up all the windows, and left the car in a mall parking lot. People in Arizona play golf in temperatures hotter than that. I had been afraid the new grill would kill me in a huge blast. Turns out it couldn't even kill salmonella. The smoker was just too big for the puny burner.

At this point, my wife came out with a plate of burgers.

"Have to admit," she said, "You were right. It looks good and seems to work."

As she went back into the house, she called out, "How long before the burgers will be done?"

I looked at the grill, my failed masterpiece, trying to calculate cooking times at 165 degrees. "Next Tuesday," I sighed. "Maybe Monday if we drive it to the mall."

Cheaper By The Yard

I have a confession. My wife and I are yard sale junkies. Each Saturday, as we drive around on our errands, we keep an eye out for those hand-lettered signs at intersections. My wife will simply point and say, "There!" and I'll make a quick U-turn to check it out.

We're not the kind of twisted fanatics who comb the papers, get up before dawn and hang around like vultures until the official start time and then swarm in and snatch all the best stuff. (Sorry. I know that sounds just a little bitter, but we've been beaten once too often. If you were really honest, you'd admit that you find those people annoying, too.) After years of experience, however, we have learned a good deal about how to get a good deal.

One rule we have come to live by is the more elaborate the signs, the lousier the yard sale. We've driven miles out of our way, lured through multiple turns by neon-colored placards, only to come to a small yard with six old dresses, a collection of romance novels (people who read them seem to buy them by the truckload) and possibly an ancient exercise bike. (There is always, I mean always, old exercise equipment.)

Another rule is not to make eye contact. When people put out a lot of signs but then offer up only the worst dregs from their basement, it's embarrassing for all involved. Usually, the family looks up expectantly as we come slowly down the street, but then their faces fall as we speed up again. We try not to meet their eyes, knowing that our failure to stop even for a moment is a devastating rejection. It's as if we're saying, "We love to spend our weekends pawing through cast-off junk, but your stuff is so awful we've rejected it from 30 yards away." It's best to keep eyes averted. I once ended up with an unwanted slow cooker just because I felt too guilty to hit the gas pedal.

We've also learned that yard sales are a great way to make the kids happy at almost no cost. The kids used to groan every time I made a sharp turn at one of these signs, until they learned better. Every yard sale has a box loaded to the brim with old Happy Meal toys, marked "4 for a Dollar."

We have piles of Happy Meal toys at home, toys that our kids never play with. But the sight of "almost new" Happy Meal toys always gets our youngest kids excited. It doesn't matter if the toy was designed to promo a movie from 1988, or is missing a head, or even if it has a mummified "Happy Meal" on it. They will play with it only for a few minutes, anyway, and next time I clean out the car, it'll go in the trash. (By one scientific estimate, America's landfills consist of almost 25 percent Happy Meal toy content.)

We've also learned not to buy from sales in our own neighborhood. You can't exactly haggle with someone you have to wave to every day over the hedge, and if you get rooked on a defective item, you'll have to hold your tongue. I still smolder over a blender with bad bearings that made margaritas taste suspiciously like burnt rubber. (We got used to them, but couldn't serve them to guests.) And it's embarrassing to put something out for the trash that you just paid a neighbor $15 for. I once drove two miles to a trash bin to throw away a high chair we'd bought from a neighbor and later regretted.

For all of our experience in this field, we don't know everything. Last year, my wife and I happened past a house where tons of great-looking stuff was laid out on the driveway. We stopped the car, got out and nodded to the homeowners, an older couple who sat in lawn chairs just inside the garage.

Their stuff was marginal, and nothing had prices, but we kept looking, hoping for that hidden treasure. After about 20 minutes, I found an old clock radio, examined it and discreetly nodded to my wife. It would be great for listening to music while I worked in the garage. I held it up to the couple.

"How much?" I asked.

The man just squinted at me through his bifocals and shook his head. "Not for sale," he said curtly.

At this I got annoyed. He'd seen how much time I'd put in combing through his load of junk.

"Then why," I asked, with just a bit of an edge, "Do you have it out here?"

The man eyed me over for a moment, then said, "We're not having a yard sale, fella. We're moving, and we're just waiting for the moving van to arrive."

The Dangling Man

This story is true. I wish with all my heart it weren't, but it is.

One recent Friday night, our next-door neighbors went out for dinner and came back around 9:30. They drove their SUV up to their side door, pulled their sleeping daughter out of the back seat and carried her up to bed. Had they looked up, they would have seen the bloody, dirty body of a man swinging from our second-story window.

It started out pretty simply. That night I decided to move an old TV into the bedroom of Son No. 2. (A privilege in our house, TVs come and go in bedrooms depending on report cards.) For this TV to work properly, I had to hook up cable. I have, over the years, routed so much TV cable around and inside my house that I should get a pension from the cable company. But I had never cabled this particular room.

Once I had the cable through the wall, I realized that I didn't have quite enough to reach the corner with the TV.

Rather than being sensible and running off to the home center (open 24 hours, cheap prices), I did what I always do, which is scrounge around the house till I find something I can cannibalize. After looking around for 45 minutes, I remembered that along the left side of the house, just outside a second-story window, I had hung some cable for a bedroom that no longer had a TV. (Son No. 1's report card last year revealed too little studying, way too much ESPN.)

It was too dark to get out my ladder, so the only way to get at this stretch of cable was by leaning out a small side window. If I stretched as far as I could, I'd be able to reach the signal splitter, unscrew the cable and pull it in the window.

At this point I should explain that we have custom storm windows on our house. We had to have them specially made, as most stock windows are inexpensive and easy to use. Our storms, however, are awkward, badly designed knuckle-busters that take at least 20 minutes to open or close, and they often get stuck halfway up or down.

I got the storm on this window up only about 18 inches, about far enough to squeeze my torso through. It wouldn't stay up on its own, so I had to prop it with the box top from the game Operation. (We have just the box top, as all the pieces were lost by 10:15 on Christmas morning.)

With the window propped open, I leaned as far as I could into the dark to unscrew the cable. What I found was that I had, in an effort to make a watertight connection, wrapped the signal splitter with about half a roll of electrical tape. So it took a good 10 minutes of fumbling to unwrap the tape in the dark. Finally, my hands covered with black adhesive from the tape, my shirt dirty from rubbing on the brick wall of our house, I unscrewed the cable and pulled.

Nothing. The connection had rusted tight. Leaning farther out, I tugged and pulled.

With the final yank, the cable separated. But in the process, I scraped my knuckles. With a loud moan, I dropped the cable line and grabbed my wounded hand.

At this point, the box top to Operation fell, and the storm window dropped like a guillotine on my back, nearly severing my spinal cord. I moaned again. Like a middle-aged Winnie the Pooh, I was unable to back through the opening, my torso swinging from the window ledge. Trapped, I tried calling out to my wife for help. She was in the living room below, engrossed in a book, and didn't answer. I yelled again.

That's when the neighbors pulled into their driveway below. I briefly considered calling out to them, but at the same time, I realized how idiotic I looked. Both my hand and my back were in incredible pain, but my ego was intact. I kept my mouth shut, dangling silently in the dark.

As they pulled their sleeping daughter from the car, she sleepily looked in my direction. I waved, my blackened hand dripping blood. She yawned and closed her eyes again. I'll bet she woke Saturday morning with a vague memory of a filthy, bloody man hanging from the side of my house and dismissed it as a bad dream.

It took me another 10 minutes to edge my way back in through the storm window. All told, my reluctance to drive less than two miles to the home center cost me almost two hours' time, my dignity, the skin off my knuckles and about a pint of blood. But at least my son now has cable in his room.

That is, until the next report cards come out.

The Revenge of Bambi

A couple years ago, as we were taking the kids up to the cabin for the weekend, we had an encounter with a wild turkey.

I was doing about 55 on a stretch of two-lane when I saw a large bird in the grass up ahead. I didn't slow down, instead calling out "Kids! Big bird on the left!" (Up to this point, I had never seen a turkey that didn't come wrapped in cellophane with a pop-up timer.)

As we got within 30 yards, the turkey jumped from the grass and took flight. This, too was a surprise to me, as I had no idea that they could fly. I still didn't slow, thinking that it would soar over our heads, and the kids would get a good show.

It turns out that while turkeys can fly, they don't do it very well. This bird only made it as high as our windshield before we met head-on. With a huge crash, it slammed into the windshield right in front of my face, spraying pebbles of safety glass across the car, leaving a turkey-shaped depression in the windshield, and causing the family dog (and at least one family member) to have an unfortunate accident.

Too late, I jammed the brakes, and as we skidded to a halt, the turkey was thrown forward into the air and disappeared into the trees. I checked and found everyone decorated with little glass bits, but OK. I had gotten the worst of it, with glass and feathers in my face and down my shirt.

The weekend was ruined, and the whole slow ride home, only half in jest, I muttered to the kids that the next time I saw that turkey, I'd even the score.

Since then, it's been a family tradition with the kids that we would take each encounter with wildlife personally, as if it were an ongoing grudge match. Every time we see a turkey in the woods, the kids scream, "Get it Daddy! Get it!" and "It's turkey sammiches for you, buddy!" Each possum, raccoon or even squirrel is met with a challenge to fight. My wife disapproves, but the kids love it.

This winter, driving the kids to the mall, we passed through a wood and narrowly missed two deer, a buck and a doe. They hopped the guardrail and ran into a little park. As we reached the entrance, egged on by the kids, I turned the car into the park. I drove along until I saw the deer hiding in the woods. To cheers of "Get em, Dad," I hopped out of the car, ran to the edge of the trees and confronted the offending creatures.

"Come on out," I called, "fight like a man!" The deer stood there, shifting back and forth, looking for the best path of escape. The kids were obviously enjoying this, so I stepped further into the woods. I was only 15 feet from the buck. I put up my arms like an old-fashioned boxer and started dancing.

"Put em up!" I called. "Let's go!" The buck eyed me warily, but didn't run.

The kids were howling with laughter, so I stepped even closer, doing my best fancy footwork. My wife finally leaned her head out the window.

"Oh sweetheart," she called out in an annoyed and embarrassed tone, "did you know that if you corner a deer, it could kill you?"

My arms still up, I glanced over at the car, where the kids had stopped laughing. They were now watching with fascination, as I suppose most of us would at the idea of seeing a man and deer fight to the death.

I turned back to the buck, who was still staring me down and who now stamped at the ground in a threatening way. I noticed now that he had a set of sharp horns, and it occurred to me that these were not merely decorative. It was my turn to freeze.

Slowly, my arms still up, I backed away, never taking my eyes off the buck. As I retreated on shaky legs, the buck stepped forward, swinging his rack at me menacingly.

Once I was safely in the driver's seat again, the kids all began to cheer. (Our 15-year-old sat with his hands over his face, presumably praying for different genes.) "You coulda beat him dad!" one twin said. I nodded, but noticed that my hands shook and that I gripped the steering wheel a little too tightly.

These days, if only to entertain the kids, I continue my little feud with the creatures of the forest. But since that day, I do it from the safety of the driver's seat.

Buy One, Get One Free

With three boys, everyone thought that we had bagged our limit. Our house didn't just bustle with activity; it was bursting at the seams. So when my wife confessed that she wanted to try one more time, hoping to get a daughter, at first I thought she was crazy. And when she later excitedly told me that we would have two girls at once, I knew we both were.

When Catherine and Olivia were born, by a harrowing C-section, they were placed in the operating room on trays next to each other. They didn't cry, but they stretched out their hands toward each other, as if they had been pulled apart forcibly.

Like most twins I suspect, they are so close that they have developed their own little world. They don't even bother to finish each other's sentences, as they've got it down to a sort of cryptic code.

One day, I passed the girls on the steps. One was bent over, looking pained. The other helped her down the steps. I stared, and then asked, stupidly, what they were doing. They looked up annoyed.

"We're playing 'Santa Claus and His Helper', silly!" they said. I nodded, watching as the one twin muttered "Ho, ho," under her breath and the other said quietly, "One more step, Santa, just one more step" It all made a certain sense. If Santa had a helper, he probably got help with everything, like getting down the steps.

A few minutes later, I walked by the front screen door to see one twin inside peering out. The other twin was on the stoop, looking as if she were about to cry. The inside twin gave out a loud "Aww, come in!" and opened the door. The outside twin came through the door, shoulders bent. Then the inside twin ran out through the door, stood with her shoulders bent and a sad look in her eye, and waited as her sister made comforting sounds and let her in.

Still curious, I asked, "Why is Santa so sad?"

They both turned around, furious this time. "We're NOT playing Santa anymore!" one snapped.

"Oh," I said, shaking my head. "Then, what, if you don't mind telling me, are you playing?"

They sighed, clearly tired of dealing with such an imbecile. "We're playing," they said together, "'Sad Person and Come In Person'" I let them go back to their game.

It would be easy to assume that because they spend so much time together they'd get sick of one another. They don't.

One day this year, we took all the kids to a crowded mall. It seemed like every family, and every kid, in the area had shown up. My wife, spying an ATM, asked me to keep an eye on the kids. As I ushered the kids to a corner, I looked down and realized Catherine was missing. A cold line ran down my spine as I realized how small she was and how big this mall and crowd were.

I began to bark orders like a general. "Go that way, Daniel. I'll take the other side!" I grabbed Jack, who didn't know what was going on, but was used to being dragged along by the collar, by the collar. "Tommy!" I shouted, "Hold Livvy's hand, don't let go, and stay under this sign!"

It was five minutes before we found her, crying in the arms of a mall policeman. She could not really talk, just blubbered really, but I could see she was all right. I thanked the policeman and headed back to where Tommy waited with Livvy.

Livvy stood ramrod straight, as if all the blood had been drained out of her. When she saw Catherine, she shivered and bolted for her, grabbing her by the shoulders.

"Tat," she said, using the baby name for her sister I hadn't heard in months. "Don't ever do that again. You are my only, only sister!" As Olivia hugged her sister tightly, tears popped out of her clenched eyes. "I thought you were gone forever!" she whispered.

The other night before bed my girls watched a news story about co-joined, or Siamese, twins who underwent a dangerous operation to be separated. The girls watched in fascination. Finally, one of them turned and asked with a frown, "Were we joined together like that?"

I looked down at the girls, sitting side by side on the couch in their pajamas, so close together they were almost in each other's laps.

"No," I said, shaking my head, "You two are joined together, but in a different way."

The Lunch Also Rises

This past weekend, my wife and I took the kids on a trip to visit friends in Annapolis, Md. On the way back, we stopped at Baltimore's picturesque Inner Harbor to show the kids a historic sailing ship, and to allow my youngest son to throw up all over the place.

My son hates long car rides. One of the ways that he copes with the boredom is to take along his Game Boy and wile away the time doing whatever it is kids do on those things. (I am praying that it's something innocent, but can't be sure. I tried once to play the thing in an effort to screen my son's activities. After three or four minutes, I gave up, as it seemed to involve nothing more than walking a stubby little cartoon character around a garden while listening to nerve-wracking music.)

At least once every trip, however, the motion of the car, combined with the inane flashing characters on the little screen, ends up causing my son's head to swim and his lunch to venture forth into the sunshine. We have made emergency stops at most of the major cities and rest stops on the eastern seaboard.

This syndrome is known among physicians as "automotive histrionic gastrointestinitus" but is known to parents across the country as carsickness. (Actually, while I did read up on the subject, I made up that technical term. I think it sounds pretty good and will continue using it till it catches on.) It stems from a "sensory overload," and seems to afflict mostly little boys and family dogs, neither of whom are capable of letting you know until it is too late.

The first sign is a weak "Oooooh!" from the back seat. Then follows a quavery "I don't feel so good!" By then it is too late, as any parent knows, as the moaning will not stop until the victim has thrown up on himself, his seat and at least one sister.

I should not be surprised. As a child, I suffered from chronic carsickness. It became so bad that my father, who did not really like driving (or living, for that matter) with children, would not even slow down when I became ill. I was relegated to the "way back" of the big old Ford station wagon, an area with fold-up seats and a mildewed smell that was clearly steerage passage in our family.

At the sound of my own nauseous whining, my father would simply yell into the rear view mirror, "Back window! Back window!" Then he would push a button on the dashboard, and the tailgate window would slide down. At the crucial moment, I would hop up, stick my head out the window, and let fly. I can still remember clearly the horrified look on the face of a man in south Jersey who made the mistake of tailgating us during one of these incidents. I could see, but not hear, his scream as he realized that the boy with the green face was interested in more than just fresh air.

I do not deal with this phenomenon as well as my dad did. Where my dad had it down to a simple flick of a switch and then a stomp on the gas pedal to clear the scene of the crime, I usually react by shouting, swerving the car, and then stopping by the side of the road and stomping up and down the berm for five minutes while my wife cleans up the car.

Still, I hope to learn from my father. Visiting family in Philadelphia this Easter, I heard the Game Boy music suddenly stop. The moaning from the third row began, and I pulled over. Having no little magic button on my dashboard, I ran back and opened my son's side window. As I pulled back on the highway, I heard the sounds of my son getting ill, and looked into my side mirror. To my horror, I saw no little face. I turned to look in the rear view mirror, only to see that he had his face pressed up against the other, unopened window. The clean-up took 30 minutes and involved almost every swear word I know.

Clearly, we have a little work to do on our system. But soon, we'll have it down pat. Be warned. If you are on the road this summer, and you see a large green SUV filled with kids, don't tailgate. One of these days my son will get it right, and oh baby, will you be sorry.

Pasta – The Food That Kills

When my 6-year-old daughter Catherine is acting up, all I have to say is "Knock it off, or Daddy's gonna make pasta!"

She actually likes pasta. (Other than peanut butter and jelly or bologna and cheese, it's the only food she will eat.) It's my making it that scares her.

It started a few months ago, when we ordered a new pasta maker. We've had them in the past, mostly ordered off of Saturday infomercials, but they have always burned out after a couple of months. This time, my wife ordered a brand of pasta maker from Italy at the recommendation of an Italian friend. This woman had been through five or six of them, but only because she seems to make more pasta than Chef Boyardee. She did, however, give us a warning. "Don't make it too dry," she said, pointing her finger at us (really, just at me).

For those who have never seen one, a pasta maker performs two functions: It kneads together semolina flour and eggs, and once the mix is just right, it is switched to extrude mode. It then presses the dough, under high pressure, through a disk-shaped die.

The pasta is really very good -- almost good enough to justify the fact that it takes about a half-hour of monotonous watching and waiting.

One evening, tired of waiting for the dough to get to the right consistency, I decided to just extrude a little after only three minutes of mixing. The dough looked a bit dry but I threw in a tablespoon of water to compensate.

As the pasta maker began to wind into extrude mode, I turned to get a plate. The motor on the machine began to emit straining noises, while at the same time, the machine housing gave off an ominous cracking sound. Suddenly, the collar on the front of the machine exploded, sending plastic flying in all directions. The metal disk shot out of the machine like a rocket, stopping only when it hit poor Catherine square in the chest. Catherine, who eats very little, weighs less than the pasta machine itself. The force of the impact knocked her off her seat at the kitchen table and flat on her back.

I ran across the kitchen, certain that I had killed my daughter and trying to remember what little I knew of CPR. My wife got there first and helped Catherine, who had a crossed-eyed, confused look on her face. My wife looked at me accusingly. "I think the pasta was just a little too dry," she said icily.

After our initial scare, we found that Catherine's only serious injuries were a round, pasta disk-shaped welt on her chest and a tendency to duck at sudden noises in the kitchen.

After that, it became the rule in our house to clear the kitchen while Daddy made pasta. Our kids came to think of the pasta maker as a menace, sort of like a countertop Three Mile Island.

Last month, as the three littlest kids sat around the kitchen table watching Nickelodeon, I gave my customary yell that Daddy was about to extrude (I know, it sounds gross) and that everyone had to clear the decks. I stood at the machine, a metal spatula in hand, ready to cut the pasta as it came out. Two of the kids reacted quickly, hopping from their seats and running into the hall. Unbeknownst to me, Catherine remained at the table, too entranced by "SpongeBob SquarePants" to sense the impending danger.

Suddenly, the pasta maker revved up, the whining motor a sign that too much pressure was building. In horror, I reached forward to turn off the motor. It was too late. With a loud crack, the collar on the die gave way, and the metal disk shot out, directly in Catherine's direction.

The disk never made it. In a stroke of (uncommon) luck, the disk hit my metal spatula and, with a loud clang, ricocheted up toward the ceiling, denting the drywall before falling harmlessly to the floor.

I turned around in a panic to make sure the kids were all OK. Jack and Olivia were peering round the corner, eager to survey the damage.

Catherine, however, was curled up in a ball under the table. I ran over, afraid that she had been hit by a piece of shrapnel. I tried to pull her out, but she resisted, crying out, "Too dry! Too dry!"

I have had no further problems with the pasta maker since that night. Mostly because we now eat store-bought spaghetti.

My Jean Pool

When my wife and I got married, I had a 30-inch waist and weighed about as much as a 13-year-old girl. But as the years retreated, so did my youthful form, and somewhere along the line I ended up with kind of body one usually finds by dragging a riverbed.

I have made periodic efforts at getting back into shape, but have seen little results. There was a period in the early '90s when I lifted weights for approximately three weeks, and once in 1997 I ran two miles without stopping once. (All right, I stopped twice. But once was for a cramped leg) As I have grown out of my clothes, some have been thrown away, but some are relegated to the top shelf of our closet, waiting for that day when I finally get in shape. The shelf has gotten awfully crowded.

To be fair, my wife has not mentioned my shape at all. (We have an unspoken treaty that neither of us will broach the subject, as it could mean mutually assured destruction.)

But in the past few weeks, my wife has slipped a number of times. One morning, watching TV in bed, we flipped to one of those half-hour infomercials for some apparatus you wrap around your stomach. When the unit is plugged in, it sends electrical shocks through your belly, causing it to contract and twitch like a frog on a lab table. Presumably, this is almost as good as sit-ups, but it looks painful and dangerous, much like the contraptions aliens used to strap on Captain Kirk all the time to torture him.

When the commercial came on this time, however, a male model appeared sporting abs with more ripples than a bag of chips. My wife took one look and said, "You're getting one of those things! Call the 800 number!" I turned in shock.

"It can cause skin burns if you don't use it correctly," I argued.

"That's okay," she said, getting out of bed. "We'll buy some Bactine."

The next time my wife unilaterally broke the treaty was at the home store. We needed an odd-shape piece of molding and asked a young employee for help. This fellow obviously spent all his time lifting cement and loading plywood, and had the body to show for it. (It didn't hurt that he was blond, tanned and in his 20s). He showed us where the molding was and walked away.

My wife stared at him (or rather his posterior) for a moment, then said, "You should wear jeans more often!"

I was about to point out to her that we both were aging at roughly the same rate, and that one shouldn't throw stones, etc., when I thought about what she had said. I had already found through trial and error that exercise was impossible, and that I could not slow, let alone stop, my rate of decay. But wearing jeans again? Piece of cake.

The next morning after breakfast, I went upstairs to get dressed. Bypassing all my baggy (and comfortable) khakis, I opened the closet. On the top shelf I found my old jeans. I looked at the tag. Technically, they were still my size, although not as "generously" cut as my khakis. (Translation: not enough space in the caboose.)

I took a pair down and slipped them on. (Actually, they only "slipped" as far as my ankles, and from there on up it was more like trying to stuff a sausage.) Once I got them on, I could only get them zipped and buttoned by holding in my stomach, exhaling, and standing on my toes.

I turned and looked in the mirror. My face was turning red, and everything that didn't fit into the jeans was now hanging over the front. Undaunted, I remembered that jeans always stretched with use, and that a just-washed pair would often feel quite loose after a couple of days of activity.

Hoping to speed the process, I started bending and squatting, pushing my rear end back and forth, at the same time shifting my weight from side to side like a sumo wrestler. With each shift, I heard the seams creak and groan, and I wondered which would give first, the pants or my appendix.

Suddenly, I looked up to see my wife in the hallway, watching my awkward "dance", a look of horror and nausea on her face.

"I was wrong," she said, wrinkling her face, "You don't look so good in jeans."

The Couch That Roared

For weeks, I had been avoiding one particularly unpleasant task. In our third-floor junk room was a huge green couch. We bought this couch at a super-sale six years ago and have been trying ever since to find a place where it might look good in our house. It sat in our bedroom for four years, but it was so piled with clothes that we never saw it. It found its way into the junk room last fall, where it's been sitting on end.

The problem with moving this couch is that it is big and rounded and offers no real place to grab onto. And because of its odd shape, it never rests properly on any one side. It just falls over, sometimes rolling but always managing to take out a lamp or two on its way down.

My wife had decided it would look perfect in our newly remodeled basement. This couch was exactly the right size, and the right color, to match the moss-colored basement walls. I offered to paint the walls a new color but got no response.

As with any major project, I spent the first few weekends complaining that it couldn't be done. When that failed, I got another two weekends' reprieve by cheerfully saying, "Sure! I'll do it tomorrow!"

Finally, I threw a fit. I pointed out that I had measured the doorway to the basement and the couch would not fit through. This didn't work, either, as my wife knows I have not measured anything in years, having lost my tape measure in early 1998. (I do spend a good deal of time yanking out drawers and yelling "Where the [blanking blank] is my [blanking] tape measure!")

The couch problem had reached the point where I had to give in. I managed to get my oldest son off the living room couch, where he seems to have made a life commitment to watching SportsCenter, and dragged him up to help me.

With me at the front end, struggling and straining, and my son at the other, standing four feet back and looking bored, we got the couch down two flights of stairs to the kitchen. On the way, we knocked three pictures off the wall, ripped six inches of wallpaper out of the third-floor hall, and cracked the glass on the door of an old china chest.

Once in the kitchen, we began trying to get it into the basement. The doorway leading there is particularly narrow and involves a 90-degree turn in a tight space. I went through first to pull and make sure it didn't fall down the steps. By Herculean effort, we wedged the front end around the corner and into the door. At this point, thinking the couch was getting heavier, I looked over the top to see my son sitting at the kitchen table, watching a baseball game and eating Doritos.

After I calmly and reasonably reminded him that he was supposed to be helping me (threatening his life only twice), we got back to it. He twisted and shoved the back end of the couch, while I tried to maneuver it through the door.

Suddenly, the couch stopped moving. I tried pushing it back out the door, but it was stuck firmly in place.

Half an hour later, after I had removed some door molding and the handrail on the stairs, I called to my son and asked him to give it one more push. Bracing myself on the stairs below, I gave a pull, and the couch slipped through the door and began sliding down the steps. I tried to slow it, but it gained momentum and threatened to flatten me. It was all I could do to keep from getting crushed as I bumped from step to step.

When I hit the basement floor, and was in turn hit by the couch, I turned to look at the top of the stairs, where my son stood, a bag of Doritos in his hand, looking over his shoulder at the baseball game.

I gave him one of those looks that, were I a cartoon, would involve steam coming out of my ears and the sound of a steam engine.

"What, Dad!" he exclaimed indignantly. "It's the bottom of the ninth!"

Later, my wife came down to see how the couch looked in its new home. "See?" she said. "That wasn't so hard. I don't know why you work so hard at putting off things!"

In Some Remote Corner...

About four weeks ago, we lost the remote control to our cable TV. I know the exact date because the remote is essential to accessing the digital cable. With digital cable, we have somewhere upwards of 1,800 channels, and the remote has 43 buttons (I counted). The front of the cable box has only three or four buttons. Somehow these few controls, none of which are labeled properly, are supposed to do the work of all the buttons on the remote. I am afraid to even touch the box. It is possible to change the channel using only the cable box, but it is incredibly slow. The move from NBC to HBO, for instance, takes around 38 minutes.

Remote controls are a big deal for me, as we have many electronic devices that I do not understand. For example, we have a gas fireplace that can be set by remote to switch on when the temperature drops below a certain point. If we misplace that remote, as we once did, there does not seem to be any way of turning off the fireplace short of dragging the garden hose in from the lawn. The TV in the kitchen seems to "forget" the cable channels every time we have a power outage. If the remote goes missing, we can't reset it, and therefore have to watch a blue screen blinking the words "Channel Set" for days on end.

There is a remote on the top of our piano that I still can't figure out. It's labeled "Panasonic," and for all I know may belong to the neighbors. I am afraid to throw it out until I find out what it's for, and will probably have it for the rest of my life.

Remotes are such crucial players at our house that I'll do anything to keep them working. I run what is almost a M*A*S*H unit for remotes, patching them up with electrician's tape and glue. One remote, now 11 years old, is so covered with tape that it looks like a hockey puck. Changing the batteries entails a half-hour operation.

So my search for the cable remote became an obsession. I looked under furniture, in drawers, and even out in the yard. I pulled out the fold-out couch, thinking it might have gotten shoved down through the mattress. I even tried all the other remotes in the house, including good old "Panasonic," in the hopes that one of them would somehow be compatible. No luck. In desperation, I stopped looking in the misguided belief that it would turn up underfoot when I least expected it. But I never stopped hoping.

Then the other day, our 6-year-old daughter sat at the kitchen table with a worried look on her face. We were watching a news report about a famous trial in which the killer received a life sentence.

"What would happen," she said suddenly, "if there was a person who thought they had broken the mote control 'cause they dropped it, and maybe they hid it 'cause they were scared?"

My first inclination was to say that they would be strung up and tortured until they revealed the location of the remote. But my wife answered first.

"Honey, they wouldn't get in any trouble!" she said reassuringly.

I added with just a slight hint of a threat, "Not as long as they told us where it was."

"Maybe," my daughter said, screwing up her face in an attempt to portray this as a genuine hypothetical rather than a confession, "the person would have hid the remote under a radiator in the living room."

I jumped up from the table and ran into the living room, dropped onto the floor and peered under the radiator. There, half covered with dust bunnies and hidden behind a forsaken Happy Meal Toy, was the remote. I pulled it out and dusted it off, examining it, like a medic, for damage. The back panel was loose and one of the batteries was missing. Other than that it was in fine shape.

I marched into the kitchen, holding the dusty, battered unit. I had been preparing my angry lecture for days, just waiting for the culprit to be exposed. My daughter sat at the table, frozen in fear, her eyes big as saucers. My wife sat at her side. "Don't worry," she said. "It's OK, honey. Daddy's not mad."

As I looked down at my precious baby, all the anger faded. "It's OK," I said. "You'll be all right. Just as soon as we get some batteries in you and find the electrician's tape."

In Hot Water

When I was a teen-ager, my father used to regularly call us all together to give us the "shower" talk. We were a big family, he'd say, with only one hot water tank. That meant that if each person took as long a shower as they wanted, the last person would be bathing in ice water. And as the last person was often my father, this was completely unacceptable.

No matter how much he yelled, it was no use. The last one up in our house routinely walked out the door in the morning with blue lips. When the situation got too desperate, my father would resort to his line of last defense, the World War II story.

My father fought his way across Africa and up through Italy, landing at Anzio. In the deserts of North Africa, water was scarce. Each soldier in my father's platoon was allowed one shower a week. That one shower consisted of 10 seconds of water to get wet, and then 10 seconds of water to rinse off. The lesson was, of course, that if my father could save the free world on 20 seconds of water a week, we could certainly get through adolescence on something less than the torrent we were using.

I tried to explain to my father the importance of my daily shower. As a high school student, I was almost like a fireman, having to be ready at any instant. (Of course, in my case, instead of a fire alarm, I was waiting for a girl to actually notice me.) So lengthy daily showers were not self-indulgent. They were just good preparedness.

My father gave me the kind of look that told me to drop it or risk losing shower privileges (and possibly the use of one arm) altogether, so I did.

Now, as a parent of five (all in one house, and all using one water heater), I have new sympathy for my father. Somehow, when I call out each morning "Please keep it short. There are a lot of people waiting to use that shower!" My kids hear, "Hey, no problem! Take your time! It's just water!"

I tried to get the kids to use my shower on the third floor, which has a water-saving showerhead. They all refused. My son Jack told me that there was so little water coming out of the shower that he "couldn't even get wet!" We also tried, unsuccessfully, to get our twin girls, age 6, to shower together. That resulted in nothing more than a five-minute shoving match as they fought for position under the spray, each complaining that the other was hogging all the water.

I even resorted to the same solutions my parents had. I went out and bought an inexpensive egg timer at the dollar store, and gathered the kids around the shower as I stepped in to demonstrate. Each child, I explained, was allowed a shower of no more than five minutes. They were to set the timer when they got in, (here, I showed them how it worked, then pretended to lather up) and at the sound of the bell ringing, (I even turned the timer so the bell would ring, making sure they knew what it sounded like) they were to shut the shower off immediately, no matter how clean they were. As with any parental talk, each child nodded dutifully, while quietly thinking of ways around the new rule.

The first morning with the egg timer, I awoke to the sounds of my two eldest boys in a knock-down, drag-out fight in a bedroom. One of them had gotten up extra early and had gotten the first shower, using every single drop of hot water in the house.

The second one up awoke to find a steamy bathroom, a pile of wet towels, and only cold water coming out of the tap. The first one, it seems, had set the timer for 50 minutes, rather than five, and had finally gotten tired of waiting for the bell to ring.

Realizing that no amount of planning or talking would help, I remembered the method my father used to solve this problem once and for all. I time each child as they turn on the shower. Then, exactly five minutes into the shower, I go into the bathroom, lean down and flush the toilet.

As I hear the sound of yelping from the shower, I smile, knowing that my dad would be proud.

Not So Many Happy Returns...

Last Friday night, my wife and I were standing in line at the grocery store's movie rental section as the couple in front of us handed over their membership card. We listened to the familiar BEEP as the card was scanned. Suddenly, the computer let out another BEEP, this one much lower and more sinister. The rest of us in line shivered; it was the warning sound that there was something wrong with this account.

The teen-age clerk frowned at the screen for a moment before declaring judgment: "Uh, I'm showing late fees of $12.54 for 'The Wedding Planner'?" The couple turned on each other in an instant. I could hear the whispering back and forth:

"I thought you said you would..." "Try taking one back yourself for once, you big..." "Oh, very mature!"

My wife and I tensed up. There probably were similar charges waiting for us, too. While we have probably rented thousands of movies over the past 20 years, I cannot recall ever returning one on time.

We start out with good intentions. As the clerk calls out "Wednesday by noon!" and passes the tape across the counter, I make a mental image of myself returning the tape Wednesday morning, hours ahead of schedule. But Wednesday comes and goes without anything happening. A week later, the tape sits on the top of our TV, gathering dust, late charges and recriminations.

We once moved 400 miles and found a rental tape from our old neighborhood when we unpacked at the new house. We had to mail it back with an apologetic note and a large check.

Somewhere in the stacks of tapes in our basement is "Basket Case," a perfectly atrocious horror movie about a young man who carries around his homicidal miniature mutant brother in a picnic basket. We rented it 15 years ago when we lived in Virginia. The late fees were so high that it was cheaper to just buy the movie from the store.

We have even avoided going back to a video store out of late-fee phobia. (You can drop a late movie into the slot without consequences, but you'll never be allowed to rent another one until you pay up.) One way of putting off the accounting is to rotate among the video rental chain, the supermarket and the local club, all in the hopes that our late fees would fall off the charts as uncollectable. (This doesn't always work. We can never go back to one place due to an unfortunate argument over a tape called "Mary-Kate and Ashley's Ballet Party," which took about 90 minutes to watch but would take a home equity loan to pay off.)

I don't mind paying for entertainment, but it seems that the movies that cost me the most are the ones I enjoy the least. The worst was a movie called "Ghost World." My wife read a good review last year and said it might be interesting. She rented it one weekend, left it in the car and forgot it until the video store called the next Thursday to find out whether we had any plans to return it.

Then, a month later, I picked it up, along with some other movies, at the grocery store. I tossed it on the kitchen counter, telling my wife that I remembered her talking about the review. She shrieked in horror, reminding me that she had already paid $14.50 in late fees for it. It remained on the kitchen counter for six days before we rushed it to the video store. Then, on summer vacation, we rented it yet again, as it was about the only tape left in the shop at the beach. I told my wife that I felt as if I had to see it, given that my late fees had probably financed "Ghost World II." (Turns out it wasn't about ghosts, the only reason I would want to see it in the first place, and I fell asleep.)

The whole thing brings on stress and guilt, two things that I like to avoid, at least on weekends. So this Friday night, I have a plan to bypass the whole issue. Instead of renting a movie, we'll gather the kids in the living room, make popcorn and settle in to watch a movie we already have at home.

I just hope the smaller children aren't too scared when that little mutant brother comes flying out of his basket with a meat cleaver....

My Family Tree

"PITTSBURGH (AP) -- Last night, in a suburb just north of Pittsburgh, only moderately successful columnist Peter McKay was killed when a huge sycamore tree broke in two and crashed through the roof above his bedroom, impaling him.

"Neighbors, many of whom were already phoning friends to let them know the house would be on the market soon, said the tree was an accident waiting to happen. Mr. McKay's editors, when asked for comment, said only that it was 'too early to tell whether Mr. McKay would be missed by the reading public.'"

When we moved to Pittsburgh and bought our house almost 10 years ago, I looked up at one of the largest trees I had ever seen. Measuring a good 6 feet in diameter and up to 50 feet tall, the tree looked like one of those redwoods in the postcards with a tunnel through it. It was beautiful, but it was right over our house.

I immediately remarked to my father-in-law that that "big hickory out back has to go." A lifelong woodworker and outdoorsman, he gave me a sad, annoyed look before informing me that

1) it was a sycamore, not a hickory

2) a tree that size would cost somewhere close to $3,000 to remove.

Seeing as I had just spent every cent I had (not to mention a couple of his) in buying the house, I made a vow to live with the tree for a while. The next time I had a few thousand bucks to spare, I'd have it cut down. (I have since come to realize that I will never, in my lifetime, have a few thousand bucks to spare.)

I have been nervous about large trees since I was a child. During an ice storm when I was 12, a 20-foot branch broke off an oak over my father's company car, a big old Buick LeSabre. It turned in the air and slammed into the front windshield like a javelin. It then ripped a hole through the dashboard, yanked the glove compartment door off and imbedded itself in the floor, right where a passenger's feet would have been.

While no one was hurt, and it was a cool thing to show off to my friends, it impressed upon me at an early age that big trees could be destructive and deadly. My parents had to call in a tree surgeon to remove the branch before the car could be driven to the shop for repairs.

Things went along OK with the big sycamore until the first winter. One particularly cold day, we heard a tremendous cracking noise outside. I looked out the window to find that it had split down the middle, as if chopped by a huge ax. I called in a tree surgeon and waited nervously for him to arrive. He came within an hour, looked the tree over and pronounced the huge split a simple "frost crack."

"It's perfectly natural," he said. "It will probably heal up in time, and you won't have a problem."

"Probably?" I asked. "What if it doesn't heal?"

"Well," he said, rubbing his chin. "The alternative is to take it down. But I wouldn't do a tree like this for under $4,000...." (At this rate, I figure, the tree should cost $30,000 in 2002 dollars to remove.)

Needless to say, we decided once more to postpone the operation. We rationalized that the tree provided shade to the house all summer, and that after all, the children slept on the second floor, with only my wife and I slumbering in the tree's path of destruction. The $4,000 would go a long way toward funeral costs, especially if the caskets could be made of freshly cut sycamore.

As the years have gone by, I really notice the sycamore only during those times when I have to rake its massive leaves in the fall, or clean up the huge sheets of bark it drops each year, or when the mess it makes clogs up my gutters (at my count, approximately every 33 days). I have even begun to appreciate its stately beauty.

But there are nights when the wind blows particularly hard, or when ice storms strike, that I lie in my bed, obsessing about the branches creaking just a few feet over our heads. I picture myself like my father's Buick LeSabre, impaled in the night, waiting for a tree surgeon to come and remove my branch. If I live long enough to get out a few last words, I will grab the tree surgeon by the collar. I will pull him close and whisper into his ear, "Some frost crack, buddy!"

Mortar Bored

Last summer, my wife decided to throw a barbecue for some friends. We had recently remodeled our kitchen and built a new deck, and we wanted to show them off. As the guest list grew, we realized that the deck could not hold everyone, and we'd have to set up tables on the lawn.

The problem was that the lawn right off the deck was not the ideal place for a party. In dry weather it was simply a dust bowl. But after even the slightest rain, it became so sloppy that it looked as if we raised hogs on the side.

So it was important that we do something about the mud patch. We'd always wanted a patio, and had been putting it off. Now was the time.

My wife, practical as always, wanted to hire a professional to pour a concrete slab. As always, I knew better. By investing sweat equity, I told her, I could put together something just as nice, perhaps even nicer, for a fraction of the cost. Although I had never worked with concrete before, it couldn't be that hard, I argued. (Believe it or not, these statements don't sound stupid to me as they come out of my mouth.)

I sat down with my wife and explained the project. I had seen these concrete forms at the home center. Using ordinary concrete and a little artistic skill, one could create a faux brick, slate or stone patio one bag at a time. I had chosen a brick look, as it seemed easiest to pull off.

Each night for the next two weeks, I came home from work, changed clothes and drove to the home store for more cement. I then spent the next few hours mixing, forming and pouring concrete. After pouring 54 bags (more than 4,000 pounds of concrete), the patio was nearly finished, with only a day to spare before the party.

I had neglected to add in the price of concrete dye, necessary to make the stones look like real brick rather than concrete lumps. At $5 a 6-ounce bottle, it was rapidly bringing the cost up to par with that of hiring a professional. (I also should have added in the cost of three shirts, two pairs of khakis and a pair of work boots, all soon coated with terra cotta lumps. The dye is incredibly messy and does not come out in the wash.)

The final step involved grouting the "joints" between the "bricks." This is done by carefully sweeping sand mix into all the joints, then watering the sand mix and letting it harden. When I pulled into the driveway with the sand mix, it was dusk. My wife stood on the patio.

"Wait till morning," she advised. "You can't do this in the dark." My wife knows nothing about concrete. (Neither do I, but that's not the point.) If I waited until tomorrow, it would not be finished in time for the party.

I carefully explained to her that if I could just point the car headlights at the patio, I could finish the job, set the grout and have no work to do in the morning. She stared at me, clearly biting her tongue, and went inside the house.

In the glare of the headlights, I poured out bags of sand mix and began sweeping. As the dust cleared, I leaned over to inspect the results. Turns out that while headlights are bright enough to scare deer, they are insufficient as work lights. I couldn't distinguish between brick and grout, and got a snoot full of dust. I kept sweeping.

Finally, an hour later, I gave up. I would just sweep and set the sand mix first thing in the morning, leaving plenty of time to set up before the party. I went upstairs, pulled off my terracotta clothes, set the alarm and went to sleep.

The next morning, I awoke to the sounds of rain on the roof. My eyes popped open, and I ran down the steps.

Outside, I found that my carefully constructed terra cotta "brick" patio was now just a lumpy expanse of gray concrete. No faux brick. Just sand mix everywhere I looked. I grabbed a push broom and tried to clean it off. No dice. The sand mix was now permanently bonded to the surface.

My wife came out onto the back deck to find the cause of all the anguished screaming. I looked up at her, waiting for at the very least an "I told you so." She just nodded and went back into the house.

She may not know concrete, but she does know me.

Dr. Daddy

It all started with a picture taken at the hospital shortly after the birth of our twin girls. Livvy and Catherine were a Caesarean birth, and as I was in the delivery room, I had to be outfitted in full surgeon regalia: scrubs, hat, and mask. Afterward, one of the nurses asked if I'd like a picture with my two new daughters, and I agreed, sitting in a rocking chair with a tiny twin in each hand.

The picture sits on the mantelpiece of the girls' room. They never noticed it until one night when I had to convince one of them at bedtime to take some cold medicine. She refused, saying that it tasted like "Burps," something I'm not sure I believed, but also couldn't argue with, as I hadn't really tasted the medicine.

Desperate, I said, "Look, I'm a doctor. And if the doctor says you have to take medicine, you do." When they both started to look skeptical, I pointed to the picture. "See," I said indignantly, "there's proof."

The girls crowded over to the frame and started asking questions. Not wanting to admit that I was lying, I quickly told them how I had been a doctor when I was younger, and that it was me who delivered them as babies. I didn't do it anymore, I said, because it was too gross and because of the cost of malpractice insurance.

That little fib got me through the medicine incident, and a few more. It also marked the beginning of my lying to my daughters to impress them. From then on, whenever I needed some authority, I would pull out some impressive but bogus achievement.

My daughters now firmly believe that I can 1) pick up a house, 2) used to be a professional football player, 3) have magical powers, and 4) was one of the Backstreet Boys. It doesn't matter what I say, as long as I say it in a confident voice, and let them know that there is a picture around somewhere to prove it. They believe it all.

I can't even keep track of the lies I've told at this point, and have had to feign amnesia at times to explain my lack of memory on certain points. My girls are constantly asking me to recount how I was, in an earlier life, the character "Woody" from Toy Story, or how I scooted down the ladder past Neil Armstrong to be the first man on the moon.

This past year, my wife attended a meeting with the girls' preschool teacher, who informed her that it was nice to meet someone with such a fascinating background. It seems, the teacher said, that the girls had told the class that they were half "monkey" because their father had met their mother in the jungle one day and captured her by throwing his yellow hat over her. It was only after Daddy brought her home and found that she was too curious that Daddy had her shaved and married her.

I laughed it off when I was told about the "Curious George" incident, as we now call it, telling my wife that it was harmless fun and that they'd grow out of it.

Last week, however, taught me my lesson. At the dinner table, we routinely ask our kids to tell us about their days at school. When we got to Livvy, she told us that today was "sharing" day at kindergarten, when everyone had to tell something about their family.

She had let the class know that her Daddy was a leprechaun, and that if they could catch him, he'd have to give up his pot of gold. I sat there staring at the table. My wife gave me a look that without a word, clearly said " serves you right, you ridiculous idiot!"

I was about to defend myself, to let my wife know that it wasn't really my fault, when Catherine interrupted.

"If you have a pot of gold somewhere," she said, frowning, "Why don't you ever share it with your children?"

I looked across the table at my daughter, so innocent and trusting, and I answered her.

"Well, we have to wait for a rainbow, honey. It's real hard to find without one of those."

We all went back to our dinners, my girls smiling to themselves, secure in the knowledge that next rainstorm, we'd all be rich.

The Whole Tooth

For years I have entertained my kids with the story of how my father pulled my loose tooth. They have now heard it so many times that when I start the tale, the younger ones groan and the older ones quietly slip out of the room.

When I was 7, one of my front teeth became so loose that it literally hung by a thread. Too scared to go to the dentist and too timid to try to loosen it with my tongue, I refused to let anyone touch my mouth.

That is, until my father got home. Concerned that I might swallow the tooth, and no doubt annoyed by the bizarre swinging fang, he marched me upstairs to a long hall lined with linen cabinets.

He grabbed a ball of twine and stood me at one end of the long hall. Reaching into my mouth, he fiddled for a minute, tying the twine to my tooth, and instructed me to keep my mouth tightly closed. Then he marched to the other end of the hall, feeding out twine from the ball. At the other end, he opened a closet door and tied the end of the twine to the doorknob. Even at my age, I had seen enough cartoons to know what was about to happen. The minute that door slammed, I was sure, my tooth, half my tongue and some of my upper lip would go flying down the hall.

At the last minute, as I stood there cringing at one end of the hall, my father straightened up, smiled and held out my tooth. He had pulled it, painlessly and discreetly, while pretending to tie in the string. As I collapsed on the floor in relief, my father walked by, casually remarking that I shouldn't be such a chicken.

While I remember it as a traumatic experience, it's one that has entertained my five kids over and over again.

Seven-year-old Jack's front tooth came out in an even more novel way. On Christmas day, we were getting ready to go Grandma's house for dinner, with half the kids in the car, when I came across Jack, still in his pajamas, playing Gameboy upstairs. It seems he had not heard my increasingly shrill demands that everyone get dressed and out the door.

I grabbed some new Christmas clothes, still with the tickets on, and rushed him into the bathroom for a quick cleanup and change. As I struggled to get his pajama top off, and as it became tangled around his shoulders, he started to yell. I couldn't understand what he was saying, but noting that he was still holding onto his Gameboy, blindly trying to save his progress, I became annoyed and pulled harder. Finally, I yanked the top free, only to find him crying, with a big gap in front where the loose tooth had been just seconds before.

I dropped down to my knees in shock. "Why didn't you say something?" I shouted.

"You poor kid!" I bent over, looking for the missing tooth in the folds of his shirt or on the carpet. It was gone. Then I looked up at my crying boy. Unable to speak because of the shock, he just pointed to his face.

"I know it's gone," I said impatiently. "I'll find it."

Jack just stared, gasping for breath. It was at that point that I realized that he was not pointing at his mouth. It was his nose. I looked in horror. Deeply lodged in his left nostril, the end barely poking out, was the lost tooth. Like some sort of circus sideshow attraction or radioactive mutant, he looked as if he had grown it there.

I quickly sat him up on the sink, and in a procedure that still gives me the shakes, used a pair of tweezers to remove the tooth from his sinus cavity. While the tooth was later placed under the pillow that night, I can attest to the fact that the tooth fairy retrieved it only with great reluctance.

Jack's rite of passage was, like mine, traumatic, but over quickly and painlessly. So while he had a few moments of horror, I know that years from now, sitting with his kids, he'll have an even better tooth story than mine. And his older kids will probably leave the room before he even gets to the part about the tweezers.

The Big Picture

When I was growing up, we had only a black-and-white television. It seemed to me that all of our neighbors, in fact the entire country, was enjoying the best of '60s and '70s programming in living color, while my family huddled around a fading, monochrome image hampered by occasional ghosts and snow.

When we asked about getting a color TV, my parents would always give the same answer: "It's just one more thing to go wrong." (Evidently, they believed that color was an accessory that one added to a set, like air conditioning or vinyl siding.)

I actually watched afternoon cartoons as a child with a pair of binoculars, peering out our second-floor window. I'd turn on the sound on our TV but watch the neighbor's color set. Luckily, the neighbor kids, Duffy and Rusty, liked the same shows we did. Unfortunately, they also seemed to stand up a lot while watching. I would sit there fuming, wondering whether I should call them on the phone and yell "Down in front!"

As I got older and got married, I was determined to get my own color set. Others may plan impressive careers or envision lasting contributions to society. I would have been happy to just be able to see a football game without a gray field. Sadly, I married a woman who is slow to warm to new technology. As late as 1997, she was heard to say, "I don't want to hear anything more about that Internet thing! I'll never use it, so I don't care!"

When my old black-and-white set gave up the ghost in the mid-'80s, we went out together to buy a replacement. I quickly found that it was going to be a pitched battle. My wife felt that watching TV was a waste of time and did not warrant a big investment. I, on the other hand, felt that lying on the couch all day in a stupor was more than a waste of time, it was a life goal.

We settled on a 19-inch model, the cheapest in the store. It was not cable-ready, of course. (We didn't have cable at the time, and according to my wife, never would.) It, did, however, have a high-tech look about it that I found very impressive. I have since realized that the manufacturer had simply painted some of the buttons orange and pasted stickers on the front. The cheaper the electronics, it seems, the flashier the look.

Now, of course, that 19-incher is getting feeble in its old age. It went through a period in the early '90s when every four or five days it gave off sparks. (It was caused, I found out by questioning the kids, by my wife overwatering a philodendron hanging over the set.)

The picture now shows a blurry band of gray for the first 10 minutes after it is turned on, and the sound cuts out at inappropriate times. My kids no longer complain, and I think now believe that that's the way televisions are supposed to operate. (Much the same way that I was shocked as a boy to watch a neighbor's set and realize that all the ghosts on our screen were from a poor signal. For years I had assumed Greg Brady was a twin.)

We went to the superstore to look for a replacement. I wandered into the aisle with the 37-inch TVs. A salesman started to explain all the features (picture in picture, stereo sound, megabass speakers!) when my wife walked up. I tried to signal to the salesman that the enemy was within earshot. But it was too late.

My wife motioned toward the set. I could see our reflection in its screen. I could see the whole store's reflection in it. I felt my heart sink.

"That thing?" she said. "You're not putting that in my living room. It's too big."

As she walked off to look at those newfangled "CeeDees," the salesman shrugged his shoulders and closed his clipboard. "I'm really sorry, sir," he said, trying to be comforting. "If it's any consolation, it happens all the time."

The only real consolation was that I remembered that my neighbors had just purchased a state-of-the-art projection television with a screen bigger than my front door. I sighed and headed off to the sporting goods department to check out prices on binoculars.

Pets Aren't Us

In a large, glass measuring cup next to our kitchen sink are two goldfish. They are, it seems, completely indestructible.

We "won" the goldfish late one afternoon from a man running a booth at a local street fair. He had obviously overbought fish and wanted badly to go home. Our kids were supposed to throw a ping-pong ball into a dish before being awarded one of these finny "prizes." But in our case, it seems they simply had to show up. Each of our four younger children, whether they hit, missed or just stood by watching, was handed a wriggling fish in a plastic sandwich bag. The fact that the man had set up his booth right next to a storm sewer made me realize that for the goldfish, there was no other ticket home from the fair.

We are, as a family, not good with pets. Over the years, we have had three dogs, none of which lasted long and each of which bit me. We have owned a hamster (squished under a rug), an ant farm (a loose lid led to a mass escape), and a series of interchangeable hermit crabs (may or may not be alive, but have not been attended to since late August).

We tried to raise a baby bird we found in the backyard this past spring. It lasted approximately 13 minutes. So, I was a little wary of bringing home another creature to what has clearly become the last stop on the highway to pet heaven.

When we got home, we poured the fish into the glass measuring cup because we had nowhere else to put them. It was not an ideal home, but I had a feeling that given our history with pets, it would be a short stay. And no matter how cramped, it was clearly preferable to the storm sewer. (That is, coincidentally, the way we look at our house: barely livable but somewhat better than the storm sewer.)

Having no fish food and with a pet store nowhere nearby, we tested various household foods to find something they could eat. We tried bread, Parmesan cheese, and even, in a bit of irony, pretzel goldfish. One day, I came in to find that someone had attempted to feed them peanut M&M's. All of it collected in the bottom of the cup as the goldfish looked out at us, silently mouthing, "NO ... NO ... NO"

Then, I tried oatmeal. The goldfish jumped at it, swallowing grain after grain, looking around for more. It was what they had been waiting for all along.

After a few days, 5-year-old Catherine's fish, the one albino in the group, died. She was told that "her" goldfish had lost some of its shine and had to go to the doctor's office to get polished up. Every few days, Catherine asked in a worried voice when her fish would be returned to the cup. I would have searched for a replacement, but the thought of driving from store to store, looking for a substitute white goldfish, seemed ridiculous.

Finally, I told her that her fish liked it so much at the doctor's that he sent us a postcard, telling us he refused to return.

Twelve-year-old Tom's fish was the next to turn belly up, but he did not seem to take it hard. When I told him of the death of his beloved pet, he simply tilted his head and said, "I had a fish?"

While I have never intentionally killed a pet, I have, through dumb luck, managed to make most vanish within at least a month. These two stupid goldfish, however, refuse to give in to their fate. At times, the water in the measuring cup gets so cloudy it looks like chai tea.

One weekend, when cleaning up for a party, we stashed them in the pantry, away from guests. We found them a week later, thinner and slightly indignant, but still breathing. During a change of water one evening, one fell in the dishwater, coming out covered in suds.

It is said that houseguests, like fish, stink after three days. These two qualify as both, and it's been 4 1/2 months. They are there each morning as I flip on the kitchen light to get my coffee, waiting for their quick-cook Quaker Oats for breakfast. I stare at them through my early morning haze, and mutter, "Just die already!"

They look back, silently but stubbornly muttering their response: "No. No. No."

I reach for the can of oatmeal, a beaten man.

Down the Drain

Like most people, I have spent my life blissfully -- and gratefully -- unaware of how our sewer system works. I knew that all over our house, toilets were being flushed, dishes were washed, and showers, long showers, were taken. I assumed, however, that everything that went down the drain disappeared, that it was just magically transported to some treatment center where it was strained, drained and filtered.

Then, as part of a basement renovation, we had a plumber come out and inspect our sewer lines. We had experienced a backup a year before, due to root infiltration, and the thought of putting carpet and furniture in an area that might at any time flood with raw sewage was too much to bear. (I use the term "raw" sewage because everyone does. If processed or cooked sewage exists, I don't want to hear about it.)

We first planned to have the line cleared only as a precaution. It was well worth the $150 to avoid damage to all the junk we call our possessions. The plumber brought a snake, a device that contains approximately 80 feet of wire and is fed by a motor down the length of the pipe. A little coil tip at the end supposedly whips around, clearing roots and "obstructions."

The plumber began the job wearing heavy gloves, but soon took them off, as the task of feeding the snake down the line was a delicate one. As the odor began to rise from the clean-out trap, I wondered aloud whether he got sick often, as he was in almost constant contact with sewage.

Neighbors of ours had once had a line back up into a closet and lived with it for two weeks before discovering the mess. They developed all kinds of sores, weeping red eyes and a chronic cough, resembling extras from the "Night of the Living Dead."

The plumber told me he was never sick, and that people are often too skittish about sewage. While I believed him about his health, I happen to think skittishness is actually a rather mild reaction to sewage.

At some point, the plumber put his ear to the trap and frowned. He said there was something "troubling" about the sound of the line when our powder room toilet was flushed. All I could think of was that the plumber now needed to disinfect his ear, too.

While most of our bathrooms feed directly into the main line in front of the house, our powder room had been added later, and the sewer line runs some 30 feet under the basement floor to link up with the others.

The plumber strongly recommended a video inspection. It cost an extra $150, but would give us peace of mind. He then hauled out a special camera setup that could film down the line. He asked me to take a position so I could view the little black-and-white screen. I did so partly because I was fascinated and partly because I had paid a lot for this show and was not going to miss it.

I stared at the little screen as the camera went down the stack and headed along the main line. Then I watched in horror as the camera slid along, past roots, sludge, and, in exquisite detail, an occasional length of standing sewage.

Suddenly, it hit me that just a foot below my feet ran a river of oozing crud, ready to lurch up any moment. I suddenly knew how the residents of Love Canal felt.

The plumber clucked a few times as the tour continued. Every few feet, roots hung from the top of the pipe, searching out the "nutrients" in the bottom of the pipe. The standing areas of water, he said, were an indication that the pipe was settling, and that we'd have further problems as time passed. In short, while we could use the powder room, the more use it got, the more problems we'd have. The solution, to put it in technical terms, was Number Ones, but not Number Twos.

As the plumber got ready to leave, he stopped short in the doorway, smiled, and offered his hand. I looked down and froze. Then, gritting my teeth in what probably seemed something like a smile, I took his hand and shook it limply.

The plumber headed toward his van, whistling a tune. I ran to the kitchen sink, holding my hand in the air, and doused it with hot water and half a bottle of antibacterial soap.

We had guests over last week, and during the visit one of them made their way to the powder room. Suddenly, my 5-year-old daughter blocked the way like a traffic cop and said, in blunt terms, "Daddy says if you gotta poop, go upstairs!"

I Stalked Bob Vila

Last week, I had to tear down some walls in the basement to make way for waterproofing contractors. As I dismantled my tool shed, I came across an 8-by-10 glossy of home repair guru Bob Vila. In a very shaky hand, he had written "To Peter -- All the Best -- Bob" It wasn't the words, but the way they were written, that made me cringe.

A few years ago, I read in the paper that Bob was going to be at my local Sears, signing autographs. I am a big fan of home-improvement shows, especially his. In my area, it ran on Sunday mornings, right about the time we were supposed to get ready for church.

While a strong believer in the existence of a higher power, I am also one of the laziest people on Earth. So Bob's show came at a particularly important time for me. I was able to point out to my wife that I worked hard all week, that I looked forward to just a few things, and watching this particular home repair show on Sunday mornings with my coffee was not really all that much to ask, now is it! (Sorry for the exclamation point, but it really sounds convincing only when I yell it.)

I drove out to Sears early that morning with my 5-year-old son. Having always thought of myself as a fairly witty person (despite clear warnings from friends and family that I wasn't half as funny as I thought I was), I spent the entire drive trying to come up with a witty remark. Finally, I hit on it. I would tell the story of how his show got me out of church, and that my excuse to my wife was that she had her religion, and home repair was mine. It would elicit a knowing chuckle from Bob, who I'm sure has a wife, too, and understands the importance of trying to get out of things.

When we got to Sears, I was shocked to find a long line, all men drawn by the prospect of meeting a celebrity. Looking around the hardware department, I grabbed a hammer. While I already had five at home, I could always use another, and besides, it helped me pretend that I hadn't come all the way out here just to gawk.

The line took forever, and the longer we waited, the more impatient my son got. His initial interest soon turned to asking, approximately every 35 seconds, when we could leave. I became more and more distracted, and felt a little ridiculous making a 5-year-old wait for 45 minutes so I could get an autograph. I leaned over and began to bargain.

A few more minutes, I said, and then we could go browse at the toy store. It quieted him down, but only for a few seconds, as he was beginning to realize that "browse" does not actually mean "buy."

Suddenly, I looked up and realized I was at the front of the line. I was face to face with Bob and a fairly serious-looking Sears executive. While Bob smiled warmly, I was immediately at a loss for words. My funny story about church could never work now. With another 50 fathers in line behind me, the idea of telling a drawn-out anecdote seemed awkward. I froze.

Struggling for words, I heard the sound of my own voice. "Uhhh," it said, in kind of a shaky and creepy tone, "I always tell my wife that ... you're my religion!" My mouth shut, and instantly I knew I'd done something scary.

Bob turned white as a sheet, staring at the unshaven, disheveled man with a hammer. The Sears executive looked alarmed and leaned forward, ready to grab my arm should I make an attempt on Bob's life. Bob reached out, and with trembling hands, asked me my name, signed the photo and handed it to me.

There was no way I could explain that what started out as a funny little story had in one second turned into a potential police incident. As I turned and walked out of the store, I noticed another Sears employee following closely behind, talking into a microphone. They watched until I got into my car and pulled out of the lot.

So Bob, if you ever read this, please know that I never intended to scare or stalk you. It was all a silly mistake, a big misunderstanding.

I'm really after that guy with the mustache from Hometime.

My Little Angel

Every morning, on my way to work, I make time to brew a pot of coffee, skim the paper, and, as I run to the bus, stop on the driveway to shovel a scattered pile of fetid trash off the driveway and back into our garbage cans.

At first, I assumed that a raccoon, possum or even rats were getting into the cans. I'd find at least one can on its side each morning, the bags inside ripped open. Things I thought I would never have to see again (corn cobs, chicken bones, now-stiff canned ravioli) spread across the lawn like the all-you-can-eat buffet in the underworld.

At first, this happened once or twice a month. Then, the attacks became more frequent. I'd try to herd the cans together, sort of gathering the wagons, but the next morning one would be culled from the herd, its guts spilled on the ground. I tried new lids. I even tried sprinkling the trash with hot sauce, something I had heard could give a wild animal a nasty surprise. It didn't work, and I now believe that tip was just concocted by the hot sauce company to make you buy more hot sauce.

Then one morning, I was up earlier than usual. I looked out the kitchen window over the sink to see a fat, aged basset hound limp up our driveway. This dog, who must have been at least 14 years old (which translates in dog years to "deceased") could barely keep its drooping jaw off the ground as it took painful step after step over to our cans.

Now, I don't really want to give out the name of the dog, for fear that the owners might be embarrassed. (Oh, all right. It's Angel, and she lives five doors down from us. The boy who owns her claims he doesn't know how she gets out, a real puzzler, as Angel is about as agile, and fast, as a bag of wet cement.)

I stood in my boxer shorts, coffee cup in hand, as Angel wheezed over to the closest can, groaned and threw her front feet up against it. Like a tree in response to the woodsman's ax, the can teetered for a moment, then fell over with a dull thump. Angel calmly walked around to the top of the can, walked in and backed out with a bulging mouthful of Hefty bag.

I ran out the back door, spilling hot coffee all over myself, and bellowed at her. Angel gave out a sad halfhearted yelp and turned to attempt a run for it. I use the word "attempt" because Angel's body seems to be about 3 feet long, and weighs somewhere around 45 pounds. Angel's legs, on the other hand, are approximately 3 inches long and seem to have no joints. Even in her prime, Angel was no Jackie Joyner Kersey.

Needless to say, I caught up with Angel about 18 inches from where she started. As I neared, Angel turned, rolled over on her back, waved her stubby legs in the air, and in dog language gave out a whimpering cry that for ages dogs have used to say "Kill me, please!"

I stopped and stared at her. Chasing a dog is no fun if the dog won't run. Hitting her was not an option, either. She was just too pathetic, and I imagine could still have bitten me on the ankles had this gotten ugly. I just stood over her and shrugged.

"Bad dog!" was all I could say. I stepped back and let Angel roll over onto her stomach and drag herself back toward the street. Ten feet on, she turned, glared at me, and gave an indignant bark. I took one threatening step toward her and watched as she instantly rolled over on her back.

Disgusted, I went back into the house. I was beaten. I couldn't seem to stop Angel, who seemed to get up much earlier than I did. I couldn't complain to the neighbors, as Angel seemed to be some sort of slow-motion Houdini who couldn't be controlled. I was out of hot sauce.

Some mornings, if I get up early, as I make my toast and coffee, I can catch a glimpse of my little Angel on her way to breakfast. I tap on the window and wave, and I swear sometimes she seems to nod, sending her compliments to the chef.

With Five You Get Heartburn

One weekend last month, on the way home from a camping trip, we stopped at a restaurant for an early dinner. Our five kids had not bathed in days and were wearing the clothes they had slept in. My wife and I were both a little tired, too.

So it was with trepidation that I led the family to a big table. Thankful for a meal that didn't include leaves or charcoal from the campfire, the kids ate heartily. Before the meal was over, the waitress came over to interrupt the chaos and leaned next to me.

"I just wanted you to know," she whispered, "that more than one table has commented on what a beautiful family you have and how well behaved these children are."

I thanked her, but was not surprised. We are constantly getting such comments from people who marvel at our economy-sized load of offspring.

As the waitress disappeared into the kitchen, 12-year-old Tommy took the opportunity to belch as loud as he possibly could. An elderly lady at the next table dropped her fork. I turned to glare at him, wishing I had access to a 2-by-4.

"What?" he exclaimed indignantly and loudly. "In some countries, that's a compliment on the food!"

I did not have a chance to answer, as at that moment, I realized that one of the twins was no longer in her seat, and no one had seen her for at least five minutes.

We have become used to the attention. Our decision to put as much thought into family planning as might the average rabbit may be a throwback to an earlier time. Perfect strangers approach us with comments and questions. The only analogy for our large family I can think of is a circus parade. It's very exciting when it comes to town, people gape at the spectacle, love the noise and flash, and wish they could be part of it. But deep down everyone realizes that there is a dark underbelly.

I envy people with one or two children. They have the time, and the strength to drop everything at the least problem. Their children are often meticulously groomed and dressed, and watched at every turn. My children, simply because there are so many of them, run wild. We seem to notice them only when they are sick, hurt or threatening to go live with the neighbors, whom they assure me are much better parents than we are.

Last week, I was on the telephone and watched silently as 5-year-old Livvy careened through the kitchen, scared for her life, closely followed by her twin sister Cat, with claws outstretched and murder in her eyes.

I simply kept my hand over the mouthpiece as Cat growled out, "I'm gonna kill you dead, Livvy!" I knew that she either didn't mean it or that she could never carry out the threat. As twins, they are pretty much evenly matched, and a fight to the death will result only in a stalemate.

None of the kids is really bad, I know. (Well, one is, but there is always reform school.) It's just that they each get one-fifth of the time, attention and guidance that a single child might. As such, where other parents might notice a child playing with markers, we don't find out about it until the girls have "decorated" themselves from head to toe.

I have come across broken dishes, disassembled lawnmowers and an entire box of Frosted Flakes poured behind the couch. Once, I came into the living room to find that an entire box worth of gum -- chewed, of course -- had been stuck to the TV screen in a smile face pattern.

Last week, watching all five at once, I became exasperated in the kitchen at lunchtime. One child was wailing, "Daddy.... Daddy....Daddy..." while I attempted to break up a fight between two others and recook a hot dog for the fifth, who won't eat "burned parts". There was a child I'd never seen before, presumably a neighbor kid, at the screen door, simply staring at me. Finally, I turned and glared at the wailer.

"What?" I said in exasperation. The child just looked at me with wide eyes.

"I just wanted to tell you," she said quietly. "I love you." She blinked once and walked out of the room.

That same camping trip last week, two elderly women approached us by the lake. They asked about the camp site and how we liked the state park. Then they got to the real point.

"You should be so proud of all these beautiful kids," one said, almost in tears. The other nodded. "You don't know how lucky you are."

I just smiled at them, realizing that they were probably right.

Into the Pit

Last week I was ordered onto my next renovation project -- finishing off our basement. As with most of our projects, this one is designed to help us shoehorn our mob of seven into a house more suited to a modern, undersized nuclear family. So we expand in every way we can, trying to get the most living space out of every square foot.

Taking on the work myself will save us so much money that I will finally be able to get the one thing that I've always wanted -- begged for actually -- but that my wife would never allow in the living room: a big-screen TV with surround sound and DVD. Moving the TV room to the basement would also mean getting the kids to spend most of their time down there, freeing up a room upstairs for other, less chaotic purposes. My youngest son asked me if they called it a rec room because it's a place kids can "wreck."

It will be a big job. Many families use their basements as TV rooms, shops, home gyms or just storage space. Our basement has been used exclusively for the past seven years as a place to ruin our personal possessions. Almost any material, be it leather, wool, paper, wood, even metal, goes into the basement dry and comes out months later ruined and covered with a thick coat of destructive mold and mildew. Much in the way that dung beetles are sometimes used to clean bones, our basement strips our possessions of all their inherent value.

The worst part is the conflicting advice. One friend tells us we will need to hire a contractor to excavate around the house and install a waterproof membrane, a monumental and expensive job. Another tells us I can coat the inside walls, made of sandstone, with hydraulic cement. A third tells us I should do nothing to the walls, and just build in from the foundation with a stud wall sheathed in a plastic vapor barrier, and just pretend the problem doesn't exist. Finally, there's my brother, who tells me that 1) hiding the dampness will cause mold spores to go hog wild, causing the entire family to choke to death in front of the big TV, and 2) I was a dope to have so many kids and that trying to hide them in the basement is just too little too late.

If the biggest hurdle is the dampness, the second is the clutter. When we moved into the house seven years ago, our basement contained an ironing board and a lawn chair. It was clean, swept and orderly. Then our junk arrived. Within a day or so, the basement was so crowded that we couldn't move. Each year it got worse. Old outdated computers, snow boots, scraps of lumber that might be useful, 15 broken fishing rods. One cabinet contains all the dishes and cups we ever owned, another 20-year-old college notebooks.

In one corner of our basement sits our "Pittsburgh Outhouse," basically an antique toilet in a shed, with no sink, no lights and no toilet paper. I open the door to the shed only twice a year, when the smell of sewage gases tells me the water in the bowl has evaporated, and the toilet needs to be flushed. Otherwise the door remains securely latched. If I wanted to go to the bathroom in a scary, dirty and slightly dangerous room, I can always go to the kids' bathroom on the second floor.

In another corner, down a little hall, is the spot where the drain backed up last summer, allowing raw sewage to spill out onto the floor. I noticed the problem only when I went back there to change a light bulb and stepped in 2 inches of oozing hell. I still have nightmares about the experience, and am thinking about putting in a claim with my insurance carrier for post-traumatic-stress treatments.

To make matters worse, the toxic spill was in the corner where we store the Christmas decorations in cardboard boxes on the floor. While many decorations survived unscathed, others had to be individually washed off, a horrifying task. I conveniently stayed late at work last year on the night we decorated the Christmas tree, and our kids were firmly instructed not to eat anything that they found in their stockings.

Between the three tons of junk, mysterious toilet, finicky sewer pipe and interesting mold patterns, I think renovating the basement will be one of the more challenging and scary home improvement projects I'll take on. But the reward of all that extra living space, and, the promise of all that electronic gear, is great. To paraphrase Arthur Miller, the basement is dark, but full of diamonds. I can already feel the floor rattle with the bass from the speakers on my big-screen TV.

Unfinished Business

I consider myself fairly handy around the house. I've renovated bathrooms and kitchens, rewired lights, reglazed windowpanes by the hundreds and renovated a sagging porch. I've even bumped out a kitchen and installed new walls, floors and cabinets.

But I have never, in seven years of intensive renovation, actually finished a job. My excuse? Supellexphobia. That's Latin for "fear of furniture."

Some jobs may actually look finished. The master bedroom is covered in red-and-green floral wallpaper that everyone tells us gives the room a luxurious, bed-and-breakfast quality. Everywhere, that is, except behind my dresser. I ran out of wallpaper, and resolve, at the end of one long weekend in 1995.

I thought at the time that I'd just finish it the next weekend. That bare spot is still there, like some telltale heart, gnawing at my conscience. I could have moved the dresser, but to do so would have meant moving all the pictures on top of the dresser, finding a place for my pile of socks, and cleaning off the scattered pennies and paper clips on top. It would have also meant facing up to the mix of dust bunnies, ballpoint pens, movie tickets and hundreds of gas receipts I knew were piled behind the dresser.

Some unfinished projects are not my fault. I renovated the bathroom on the third floor in 1998. I moved the tub, replaced the toilet and sink, tiled the floor and put up chair rail. I even wallpapered the whole room. One corner, though, remains unfinished. All it needs is a few feet of baseboard, maybe a little quarter round. But before I could put on the finishing touches, my wife put her foot down.

The marble top, chair, blanket chest and table that belonged in the bathroom had been sitting in the hall for at least four months. She just had enough of squeezing by the furniture in the hall, and moved it all back into the bathroom. Now, finishing the bathroom means I'll have to move the marble top away from the wall. The marble top, in turn, is piled high with bath soap, trays of earrings, assorted cuff links and a two years' stack of home repair magazines.

Suddenly, a little carpentry has turned into a major housekeeping job. So the baseboard remains unfinished. I barely even notice, even when my wife asks if I'm ever going to finish the job. The gap between the tile and the wall has turned out to be a good place to sweep the dirt when the dustpan goes missing.

In the dining room, I put together some fancy wainscoting to dress up a rather plain room. On three sides of the room, the wainscoting features a chair rail and wooden box molding. On the fourth wall, it features only a chair rail. The culprit? A sideboard which weighs more than a 1969 Volkswagen Beetle. While I'm sure that I could move it, to do so seems a little risky. It contains literally 1,700 pounds of old china, glasses, pieces of eyeglasses, Easter candy from 1997, brochures for beach rentals, maps, and, for some reason, one of my old dress shoes. Moving the sideboard means either breaking a lot of china or emptying it out. So the point is moot.

Everywhere I look, there are reminders of my inability to move any object heavier than a plant stand. The old wallpaper in my wife's home office has been stripped, at least in some places. The living room is painted a soothing charcoal gray -- except behind the grandfather clock. The clock is not only heavy, but needs to be leveled when moved. (Not gonna happen.)

My wife and I have learned to live with my unfinished projects. When you spend enough time with something, or someone, you learn to live with what at first seems to be major shortcomings. My house, flaws and all, has become an extension of who I am. And just the same way that I have come to terms with my thinning hair and jug ears, I've become comfortable with my house's little faults.

Some day, when we die, some buyer will look at the place and wonder what kind of idiot could walk away from so many projects in midstream. Perhaps I should leave him a note. It'll just say "supellexphobia." I'll write it on the wall behind the sideboard. If they're anything like me, they'll never see it.

Off With Their Heads!

During a recent kitchen renovation, we put in a number of upgrades, including new counters, cabinets, dishwasher and, most importantly, an 800-pound mousetrap.

The mousetrap doubles as a refrigerator. When it arrived, we marveled at the ice maker, the side-by-side doors and sleek lines. What we didn't know, and what the manufacturer does not advertise, is that underneath the fridge, right about the height of a small mouse, is a metal fan. This fan is used to cool the motor under the fridge when it gets too warm, and it sits an inch-and-a-half above a small metal drip pan.

Mice, it seems, love to hang out in warm little spots like the drip pan. And if they are curled up in the pan taking a nap, it seems only normal that at the click of the fan motor, they will raise their little heads to see what is happening. The inevitable result is one that the Queen of Hearts might find amusing, but that I find disturbing, to say the least.

I first found out about this problem when I noticed a strange smell in the kitchen. At first, of course, I assumed that it was my 10-year-old, who was sitting in the kitchen eating an entire bag of Fritos, and who doesn't seem to understand the concept of hygiene. Then I realized that it was coming from vicinity of the fridge. Some leftover Indian food had finally begun to mold, or juice had spilled in the bottom of the tray, I figured. We cleaned out the fridge, assuming that the problem was solved.

Within a week, however, the smell had become overpowering and was clearly the odor of "something that had been alive at one time but is no longer."

I moved the fridge away from the wall, exposing all the usual debris. There were a few fridge magnets, some stray Cheerios and Kix, my youngest son's spelling words that had been the subject of a frantic search the month before, and a dust bunny or two. I kicked aside one of the dust balls, and got on my hands and knees with a flashlight to see what had happened.

That's when I came upon a scene so horrifying that fuzzy black-and-white pictures of it will one day grace the center pages of a true crime book by Ann Rule. In the drip tray was the torso, and nothing but the torso, of a small brown mouse. It took me a few seconds to focus and realize just what I was faced with.

A chill ran down my spine as I slowly turned my head and examined the "dust bunny" not 3 inches from my face. Two black little eyes stared back, a look of surprise and horror on the furry face. I scrambled to my feet, gagging and wincing. What followed was five minutes of the children crowding in for a look, running away screaming, and then coming back for another peek.

The cleanup was made worse by the fact that I had not acted more quickly upon noticing the smell. While a freshly killed mouse may be cleaned up with a dustpan or flipped into a paper bag, suffice it to say that a week-old mouse corpse cannot be cleaned up without a least half a roll of Bounty towels, rubber gloves and a clothespin on the nose.

I moved the fridge back with a shudder and waited. Sure enough, six weeks later the smell returned, and I quickly moved the fridge out of the way to remove the next victim. It has happened twice more since then.

It seems there is nothing I can do about this problem other than, I suppose, suing the manufacturer over this design defect. Its defense would be, of course, that I am not a close relative and am therefore not able to collect for the injured party.

The whole point of the kitchen renovation was to have a place where the family could gather, where we could sit and relax together over a cup of cocoa or a bowl of popcorn.

It is all that, of course, but only until the next time the whir of the fan starts, we hear a muffled thump, and a small, gray dust ball comes rolling across the kitchen floor. As the children run from the room screaming, it feels more like dinner time at the Addams Family's.

The Lawn, Hot Summer

I live for one week a summer. It's that one stretch, usually when I'm at work, when the lawn looks perfect. It happens in mid-June. Before that time, the lawn is a dry, brittle expanse of last year's dead grass, this year's weeds, and shards of children's toys the dog has worked over.

After that time, the summer sun has had a chance to work its magic, and the lawn is burnt out, thin and brittle. But for that one week, that one glorious week, I have a dream lawn. But it's just one week. My neighbors enjoy luxurious turf straight through from April to September.

It's not that I don't try. It's just that I'm afraid of the chemicals. People who understand the use of fertilizers always warn that there's a real danger of burnout. One neighbor, whom I like to think of as the Yoda of lawn care, warns me repeatedly in his raspy voice:

"If you put too much fertilizer on, you turn your lawn into a toxic waste site, where nothing, not even a weed, will grow. And that spot will remain barren, for all eternity. You might as well put in one of those Japanese sand gardens."

It sends a chill down my spine, and I believe. So I always skimp on fertilizer.

This year, I decided to start early, and put down some grass seed and fertilizer in early April. I carefully picked "starter" fertilizer that would not burn out the new seedlings. I applied seed and fertilizer according to directions, and then sat back to wait. It was a long wait.

Soon, my neighbors' lawns started to come up, most of them so thick and verdant that it looked as if you could eat them. My lawn just sat there, seemingly in a coma. People would walk their dogs on Saturday afternoons, and as they'd pass our house, they'd nod toward our lawn.

"Poor idiot," they were probably thinking. "Hasn't he ever heard of fertilizer?"

I wanted to chase them down the street, explain all the measures I'd taken this year, how hard I'd tried. But I did the next best thing. I jumped into the car and drove at top speed back to the hardware store where I'd bought the fertilizer. Luckily, a rep from the Brand X fertilizer company was there, consulting with customers over the best lawn "system" to use.

As I waited my turn for a few drops of lawn-care insight, I listened as other homeowners described their various lawn problems.

To each seeker of wisdom, he offered the same advice. "I'd buy Brand X fertilizer. It's right down at the end of the row. And don't forget to buy our spreader." (The fact that he works for company X has nothing to do with the advice he was giving. And the fact that there was a huge overstocked pile of Brand X fertilizer at the end of the row was also irrelevant, I'm sure.)

I explained my situation. I had followed directions but still had a brown lawn, while all my neighbors displayed lawns that looked like Astroturf. My lawn looked as if it ought to have a chalk outline around it and police photographers milling about. He eyed me up and down.

"That's because you used starter fertilizer," he sighed, as if talking to a child. "That doesn't promote greening. It just builds roots. You won't get much greening," he assured me again.

It took a moment to process this. "But 'greening' is what I want." That was the only point of fertilizer. "I don't care about the roots. My neighbors can't see the roots."

He just shrugged his shoulders. "If that's the case, you should have used ..."

"I know, I know," I said, cutting him off. "Brand X fertilizer."

"Sorry," he said, shaking his head. "You've already fertilized. You do it again, and you'll get burnout."

I tried to argue, but he made it clear that Oz had spoken, and there were others waiting to pick his brain. I was dismissed.

I waited, skulking about the rakes and shovels, until he took his break. Then I grabbed a cart, ran over to the end of the row and loaded up bags of Brand X. I took it home, spread it over the lawn, and sat back on the porch with a beer to wait.

I don't fear burnout any more. If it comes, it comes. Besides, I'm too busy planning my Japanese sand garden to worry.

The Max Factor

A year or so ago, I happened to walk through a local department store during one of their periodic dog shows. This was an annual event where the dogs were outfitted with big bows, groomed carefully, and trotted out like little Oliver Twists looking for a home. It was bad timing. My oldest son had been bugging us, nonstop, for a dog. His need for a dog had reached the point of obsession.

Dizzy was some sort of sheep herding dog. Alert, calm, affectionate, he was everything you could want in a canine companion. This was the dog.

The next day, Saturday, we took the kids to the shelter with the idea of bringing home Dizzy. To our dismay, we found a little sticker on Dizzy's cage indicating that he had already been claimed. The children were heartbroken, and my wife and I, in a moment of weakness, began looking at the other dogs.

That's when we came across the cage of a dog I'll call Buddy. I cannot reveal Buddy's real name, as I've checked recently, and he's still at the shelter. I do not want to ruin Buddy's chances of ever finding a home.

While Buddy was not particularly good-looking, he did have one good quality. He was available. Buddy had been adopted before, but returned, with the excuse that he needed more attention than the previous owner could devote. We took Buddy for a test walk, during which we were told that Buddy was good with children, housebroken, and never barked. While he wouldn't sit or heel on command, he could at least fetch, part way. When one of our children threw a ball across the yard, Buddy would follow the ball, pick it up, and walk away with it. We figured we could work on the "returning the ball to us" part later. We took Buddy home that day, and renamed him "Max."

The first step was confirming that Max was, in fact, housebroken. In reading up on dogs, I found that dogs have a natural aversion to peeing in their own nesting area. Their instinct is to pee as far away from the family home as possible so that predators, such as cougars or bears, won't be led back to the nest. The trick, of course, is to make them understand that the "nest" is the house, and that the yard (or preferably, the neighbor's yard) is the proper place to do their business.

Max did not catch on to this concept. Max saw our house as one big water closet, and seemed to make it his goal to go everywhere at least once. Everywhere except on the lawn. I could stand outside for 20 minutes, chanting "Go Potty, Go Potty," until I turned blue, and then watch him trot inside to raise his leg against the kitchen cabinets. He had a particular fondness for my daughters' bedroom, which had a white carpet. I came to think of him as almost an artist, like a subway vandal with a spray can. He was making his mark. All the talk about instinct and "keeping the nest clean" now seemed somehow funny. Had we lived in the wilderness, I expect within three or four days, I'd wake up to find a hungry bear or cougar at the bottom of my bed, gnawing at my foot.

Max also was not good with children, it turned out. I once found our 3-year-old daughter frozen against the wall, with Max staring at her. From deep inside Max's scraggly body, I heard a low throbbing growl that I imagined could only have come from Cerberus, the three-headed guardian of hell. Later that afternoon, that same daughter had the misfortune of coming upon Max right at dinner time. Without hesitation, Max jumped up, bit her on the nose, and went back to his meal. It was the final straw.

That night, we gathered the children around the table to inform them Max had to go. A few cried. One didn't seem to even realize we had a dog. And the little girl with the bandage on her nose just looked relieved. As I spoke, I saw Max glaring at me from the hall. Our eyes met, and right there I knew that Max had been in this situation before. The serious family conversation was a signal to Max that the jig was up, it was back to the slammer. Max was the Robert Downey Jr. of the canine set.

Max gave me one final glare, and then turned to run up the steps. Knowing what was up, I sprang from the table and raced after him. When I finally reached the third floor, out of breath, I found Max exacting his revenge. I had just gotten my favorite suit back from the cleaners, and had hung it from the bedroom door, not wanting to get it wrinkled in the closet. There was Max, looking gleeful and peeing right down the front of the suit. It was all I could do not to strangle him right there in the hall.

The next morning, I drove Max back to the shelter, where he was led back to his cell, like Steve McQueen in "The Great Escape."

A year later, I walked through the department store again, and saw the sign for the animal shelter. I heard a lady saying "he's good with children, he's fully housebroken and he's..." The rest filtered out into crowd noise. Then I heard the words: "His name is Buddy." I stopped and turned. There, sitting on the floor with a wide canine grin on his face, was Max, my old nemesis. Our eyes met, and I considered turning him in. I'm not sure if he recognized me, or the suit. But I swear he raised an eyebrow at me, challenging me to come close enough so that he could raise his leg. I kept walking.

I really do wish Max well. I just hope whomever adopts Max next has the sense to hang their suits up on a high hook.

The Fastest Gun in the House

After a year of talking about it, I finally gave in to my wife's pleas that I construct built-in bookshelves, window seat and cabinets on the first-floor landing.

Our house, a brick Colonial with Federal accents, sports a lot of molding and decorative brickwork on the outside. But it's surprisingly spare inside, as if the original owners ran out of money halfway through building the house in 1919 and in a panic ordered that the entire interior be trimmed only in 1-by-4s.

This might be fine for some, but it does not fit in with the image I have of myself as a Renaissance man living in the midst of Old World charm. I've spent a good part of the past seven years trying to spiff up my surroundings, with chair rails, wainscoting and ornate dentil molding. Especially dentil molding. (My feeling is that any project, whether it's shelves or a mantelpiece, looks fancier with a strip of dentil molding across the front. I'd even put it on my car if I could find a way to get it to stick.)

But I'd never actually built anything. I'd tacked molding onto everything that didn't move, put down floors and replaced toilets. But I'd never taken on building something that would stand on its own, something that might be considered more as a piece of furniture than as a decoration.

Every amateur handyman or builder knows the adage, "Cut once, measure twice." The idea is that you should proceed carefully and thoughtfully, putting sharp metal to wood only once you've determined exactly where to make your cut.

My credo is a little more complicated. It's "Measure three times. Don't write measurement down because you have such a good memory and are so darn smart. Find saw. Come back and start hacking away. Realize that you have failed to mark and/or cut properly. Swear like a sailor. Throw tape measure."

The first time this happened to me, I was horrified. My first set of built-in shelves were a quarter-inch short. I swore that I'd try next time to measure more carefully, to take my time and to cut along an exact line. With patience and determination, I could perfect my technique and become a craftsman. But first, I'd have to disassemble the shelf I'd just painstakingly nailed in place and start from scratch, meaning a return to the home store for more supplies.

That's where I discovered caulk. It is a creamy white substance that looks like toothpaste and smells like hell. It is applied with a really cool-looking gun that you can hang on your belt and which makes you look like a tough guy. (Rather, it makes me look like a tough guy. Try it at home alone before wandering out in public. It might not work for you.)

Caulk is sold in home stores by the truckload. Hundreds and hundreds of these missile-like tubes line one aisle, with customers snatching them by the armload as if they were rare Beanie Babies. It seems the whole country must be awash in caulk.

I now know why. Caulk makes mistakes disappear. Once home, I tiptoed back up the stairs to the scene of the crime.

After a quick glance over my shoulder, I drew my gun and fired. In a few moments, the quarter-inch gap between shelves and cabinet was obliterated.

The shelves were to be painted white anyway, and I had no intention of taking them down before I moved. By the time someone discovered my little shortfall, I'd either be retired in Florida or under 6 feet of solid earth.

Soon, however, it got out of hand. If caulk could mask a sloppy cut, it could easily bridge the gap between the wall and the window seat, a sign of poor planning. It could cover spots where a nail had bent on the way in and I had just crushed the head down sideways in frustration. If I squeezed it onto my fingertips, I could smooth out virtually anything.

After an hour or so, I stepped back to admire my work -- and gaped in horror. There was so much caulk smeared on the project that it was starting to resemble a huge poisonous birthday cake. It was no longer a woodworking project; it was now a free-form sculpture. Empty tubes of caulk littered the hall like spent gun cartridges. Not even the fancy strip of dentil molding could make this look right.

I knew something had to be done, and quickly. My wife would soon be up to check on my progress. I ran to the basement and grabbed a can of all-purpose white paint. Loaded up with pigment, it would be impossible to tell wood from latex.

A second hour later, I stepped back just as my wife stopped by to inspect my handiwork.

"You did that?" she asked, cocking her head and squinting. I waited nervously. Then she nodded slowly. "Pretty impressive! Didn't know you were so talented!" I beamed as she went back down the stairs. I couldn't tell whether I was happy or simply dizzy from the smell of all that curing latex.

Every time I pass that landing I look up, feeling proud, guilty and relieved. Proud because I managed to put together something that, from a distance at least, looks pretty impressive. Guilty because I know that under all that gleaming white paint is enough caulking to have kept the Titanic seaworthy. And relieved because no one knows this but me. I even get compliments on my handiwork, which I accept with an "aw, shucks" kind of shrug.

I found in the end that caulk doesn't make your mistakes go away. It just hides them from the rest of the world, giving you the appearance, at least, of competence. And sometimes, that's good enough.

The Big Chill

I read recently about a hotel in Canada made entirely of ice. Visitors can spend the night sleeping on a big block of ice (albeit with plenty of covers), sit on frozen chairs, eat at frozen tables and drink iced vodka.

But Canada is awfully far away. If you like this sort of thing, I have a better solution: Sleep in our master bedroom anytime in the next two or three months.

The idea of moving our master bedroom up to the third floor was mine. But, like more than one of my renovation ideas, it was ill conceived. Our house is not small, but with five kids, there were times when we seemed to be bumping into each other every 10 minutes. The third floor, used only for storage, offered room for expansion.

We knew when we purchased the house that the third floor had been set up as an apartment in the 1940s. But back then, the room had a gas heater hooked up and was probably quite toasty. The gas lines in our house had been cut decades ago, and the cost of running radiators, or any new heat source, up to the third floor was prohibitive. It didn't matter, though. I convinced myself that if we kept the third-floor door open, enough heat would rise from the rest of the house that the third floor would stay reasonably warm.

We started the renovation in the fall. I gutted the 1930s bathroom, moved the tub across the room, added a shower, and installed a new sink and toilet. I carpeted the bedroom, painted weathered old woodwork and wallpapered. Within a few weeks, this former storage space began to look like a bedroom suite out of House Beautiful. We moved upstairs to our getaway, smug in the idea that we had added so much living space at so little cost.

Then the weather turned colder. The first few brisk nights, I went to bed in a sweatsuit. As the cold wave continued, I moved on to a knit cap and threw on so many wool blankets our bed looked like an Indian trading post. One morning that first winter, I had to clear ice off the inside of the bedroom window to see outside.

I had begun to identify with George Leigh Mallory, the Mount Everest climber who got lost in 1924 and whose frozen body was discovered only recently. With minimal equipment, he and a friend ventured too high and paid a terrible price.

We survived the first winter, however, and five since. While I am still not completely happy living like an Eskimo, I have adapted. Now, I can feel comfortable in anything more than 54 degrees. I know because we have a little thermometer mounted in the bathroom. When it hits 52, I stop taking showers on the third floor. It's hard to shave when your teeth are chattering.

On mornings when the mercury stays under 50, I simply jump out of bed and run for the stairs, not coming back up till it's time to get bundled up for bed.

The only thing worse than living on an unheated third floor in the winter turns out to be sleeping there in the dog days of August. A slate roof, while beautiful and long-lasting, also soaks up heat all day in the summer sun, and then radiates that same heat down into the house all night. A fan on the ceiling doesn't help much. It works instead much like a convection oven, in which the hot air is circulated over the food by a fan, rapidly reducing cook times. Were I a Butterball turkey, my little red temperature gauge would pop out before 2 a.m. on particularly hot nights.

My wife and I comfort each other by saying that this kind of hardship builds character, that what doesn't kill you makes you stronger. Neither one of us wants to be the first one to bail and ask to sleep on the fold-out couch downstairs. But some nights, as I lie in the dark shivering and watching my breath float in the air in a little cloud of steam, I wonder.

Maybe I could slip downstairs, warm up by the fire and send a search party for her in the morning.

Withering Heights

I am a man with a price on my head. That may sound very exciting and dangerous, until you find out the price -- $1,789. In other words, the cost of replacing one of our gutters.

I'm usually pretty brave about taking on home projects. But I've always had an aversion to climbing tall ladders. It may stem from a summer spent painting houses with my brother, when I was the lightest (and weakest) person on the crew. It was always my job to climb to the top of the tallest ladder when we had to work on soffits or eaves of particularly tall houses.

The theory was that I was too weak to hold the ladder for my much more solidly built older brother, and my brother, in turn, was too heavy for the third-hand, slightly dented aluminum ladder we were working with. It was nerve-wracking, but I was young and stupid.

But in recent years, as my responsibilities and income have grown (the former at an exponential pace, the latter at just about the cost of living), I've made it a point to avoid situations that might transform me from a family provider into a chalk outline. For the past seven years, we've always had others work on our roofs and gutters. The theory here was that I was too valuable a member of the family unit to risk on such a dangerous job, and that other family members (wife, kids, dog) were either too small, scared or smart to climb a 30-foot ladder.

This policy held up until our recent gutter leak. Our house may not be big, but it's tall. Really tall. I've been up there once, on a borrowed ladder, and it was a heart-stopping experience. My knees were shaking so hard that the entire ladder rattled. I was up there just long enough to picture the film clip on the evening news as they carted my body away in a red velvet bag. I haven't been up there since.

So I called our local roof and gutter man. After he took a look, he came down shaking his head in the serious way that such men do when they are about to offer a very serious estimate.

"Whole box gutter's got to be replaced," he said mournfully. "You need to have the box rebuilt, the gutter relined, and you need a membrane under the first three rows of slate."

He looked quite sad. He ought to be an actor because I know for a fact that this was not a sad thing for him at all. In fact, it was a very good thing for him. Then he gave us the bill: $1,789. My wife and I just nodded, both of us trying not to whimper in the presence of a stranger.

After the roof and gutter man departed, no doubt chuckling and mentally spending my next paycheck, I turned to my wife in shock.

"For that much money," I said, half in jest, "I'd climb up there and do it myself. I don't care if it kills me."

My wife looked me straight in the eye.

"You're darned right you will," she said. "Go buy a ladder."

She patted me on the shoulder and marched into the house.

We all question how much we're worth, what kind of impact our passing will leave on this earth. I found out that day that I am worth approximately $1,789, and that the impact I will leave is probably going to be a 5-foot-11-inch crater in my front yard.

Mulch Ado About Nothing...

I hate the fall. To many people, it means crisp nights, beautiful colors, trips to the local farm market. To me it means leaves. I feel about leaves the way the Grinch felt about Whos, or the way Mr. Wilson felt about the little blond brat next door. I like raking leaves the way a cat likes a bath. They are a major strain on my normally easy life.

I grew up in a house of nonrakers. Two of my brothers worked on a grounds crew at the local country club. As such, they had access to a leaf blower that was strong enough to turn over a small car. Once a year, usually in early November, they'd steal the leaf blower from the club, bring it home, and blow all our leaves, a whole season's worth, off the lawn. The leaf blower was so strong that it blew a good portion of the leaves straight across the street and on to the neighbor's lawn, something I thought was pretty funny as a kid, but now realize could lead to gunfire. My brothers were always quite proud of the fact that they'd saved a whole season of work. The message I grew up with was that leaf raking was for chumps.

That's why this season always creates a little tension in our house. My wife grew up in a house where leaf raking was not just a necessary chore, it was a moral imperative. My wife's family sees a leafy lawn as a sign of lax morals on display for the whole neighborhood. Like a recycling bin full of whiskey bottles, or a sheriff's sale notice tacked to the front door, piles of leaves tell neighbors there is something not right in this house.

My solution was, I think, ingenious: a mulching mower. A mulching mower is designed to cut up bits of grass, the odd leaf, and small twigs into tiny little pieces. These pieces, as they decay, fall into the soil and become fertilizer for the lawn. I have read that after two seasons of mulching, a homeowner can develop such healthy soil that he/she can dispense entirely with fertilizers.

The logical conclusion, of course, is that if a mulchified leaf or blade of grass is good for the soil, 6 inches of leaves, all cut up at once, would be like a power breakfast for my lawn. So, for the past few years, I have simply mulched my leaves away. If the mower could handle scattered leaves, I figured, why not wait until the leaves got a little heavier, and then plow on through? It's amazing how my mulching mower, if pushed to the limit, could decimate what at first seemed to be a virtual Mount McKinley of leaves.

It turns out that the mulching mower was able to mulch things other than leaves, as well. Like a Barbie. Or a yo-yo. A summer issue of Vanity Fair. And once, a kid's shirt, abandoned in the back yard when the weather turned hot. All fell before the mulching god, shredded into little pieces that, with a little time, faded into the soil of my lawn. Not exactly good for the soil, but probably not too bad, either.

Then one day last fall, the mower finally gave out, choking to death on a 3-foot-high pile of leaves and twigs. I was left to stare, slightly shocked, as a little plume of black smoke rose from the engine and a trickle of dirty oil ran down the driveway. After that, the mower still started, but wheezed out after a minute or so. It is as if the poor thing had lost its spirit.

I haven't had the heart to get it fixed, as any repairman would take one look at my mower and ask whether I'd been using it for illegal purposes. The bent blade and chipped body are hallmarks of "one who does not care properly for one's tools." So all summer long, my mulching mower has sat in a corner of the garage, rusting, and I've just borrowed my father-in-law's mower.

It's been fine all summer, especially because my oldest son is now old enough to cut grass, and is the one who has to bear the shame of pushing around a borrowed mower. But now the trees are turning, and what started as a trickle has grown into the inevitable autumnal avalanche.

I sit on the side porch, watching as the leaves get deeper and deeper, and wondering if my father-in-law's mower has a mulching blade.

Up Against the Wall

I've tackled a lot of home projects before. Some were minor, some were ambitious. Some were beyond my admittedly limited abilities. But this time I'd really done it. I leapt, without even a hint of a look. I'd bitten off more than I could chew. I'd rushed in where no angel would ever tread.

Our kitchen was small, so small that when all seven of us sat down to dinner, I didn't. I usually leaned against the stove, trying to balance a plate and glass, all while fighting off the dog, who clearly had an interest in making me spill my dinner. Four of the kids were crowded around a tiny table crammed into a corner, with one more perched on a stool on the other side of the room. I had seen bigger kitchens in fold-out campers.

Our kitchen plan seemed almost amazingly reasonable at first. Behind our kitchen was a porch. The house is made of solid brick, and the porch is as well. It actually supports a bedroom upstairs.

If I enclosed the porch, I reasoned, and took out the brick wall between the two rooms, we'd have a huge eat-in country kitchen, big enough to hold a long kitchen table with room for all seven of us at once. We'd have plenty of room to spread out. No one crying that they'd been knocked off the bench. No one shouting that he won't sit next to So-and-So, who makes disgusting noises when he chews. (He does, actually, which is why I call him So-and-So.)

I spent months trying to convince my wife that this really could be done, and that I was the man to do it. I showed her floor plans, elevation drawings and perspective drawings, all scribbled on legal pads. Never mind that my perspective drawing had a little too much perspective, making our kitchen look as if it was being sucked into a time tunnel, and that my drawing made a solid brick wall disappear, without an explanation as to how it would be done.

After months of prodding, she relented, but only, I suspect, because she had found a long kitchen table she really liked, one that would not fit in our original kitchen.

I enclosed the porch last fall. I ripped out the old porch floor, dug a foundation, laid floor joists and a plywood floor, then put a set of windows and french doors into the two openings in the porch. In a matter of weeks, I turned a decaying old porch used only for collecting junk into a drafty, dirty little room with an uneven floor that at least hid our junk from the neighbors.

But as warm weather approached, I began to have second thoughts. The next step was to remove the wall. What had looked so easy when sketched out on legal pads now seemed ridiculously complicated. I'd have to first relocate the sink, dishwasher, stove, cabinets and microwave. To do that, I'd have to move a radiator, run new gas, water and drain lines and add at least five electrical circuits.

Given the fact that I knew nothing about plumbing, heating or electricity, this was shaping up into a major problem. But there was no way out. By enclosing the back porch, I had committed myself.

Throwing caution to the wind, I attacked the demolition with hammer and crowbar. Within minutes, I had opened up a hole in the ceiling large enough to stick my head into. The first shock came when I looked at the joists. Without the wall underneath, the entire ceiling, and probably most of the bedroom above it, would come crashing into our kitchen. It was, I learned, a "load-bearing" wall, which ranks up there with "rabid raccoon" and "third rail" as things one should not mess with. What's more, the ceiling was strung with a web of twisted and cracked old wires held together by black tape. One wire, in fact, was resting on my forehead, ready to deliver 110 volts at my slightest move. Horrified, I slowly and carefully pulled my head out of the hole.

The next shock came when I climbed down from the ladder. The little patch of ceiling I'd pulled out, maybe only 2 feet square, had dropped a black cloud of sticky coal and plaster dust over everything in sight, including most of our food and two of our children. They had been sitting at the table eating lunch and now looked like little coal miners on a break. It took most of the afternoon to scrub up the mess, throw away the ruined food and hose off the two kids. It took two full days, however, for my wife to talk to me.

With that, I had to admit defeat. I called in a contractor, electrician and plumber. Turns out I was not the man to do the job. I was only the man who hires the men to do it.

The contractors came in and made short work of the job. In just weeks, the old walls were out, thick beams were in place, wiring and plumbing were roughed in and bright new drywall covered everything in sight. We finally had a kitchen big enough for everyone to have a seat at the table, one with enough room for "So-in-So" to sit off by himself so no one has to hear his chewing noises.

Contractor for a Day

I've always wanted to be a contractor. I want the big pickup, the paint-spattered boots, the banged-up radio, the lunch pail with a big hoagie and the Thermos filled with lousy coffee. I like contractors. But contractors don't really like the rest of us. They think we're silly, stupid, lazy fools. They are happy to take our business, but they really don't like talking to us about their work, because they know we don't know what we're talking about. I know this for a fact, because for a few brief, shining minutes recently, I was one of them. Or at least they thought I was.

I was at the local home improvement megastore, buying some lumber to finish my deck. One particular piece was a 6-by-6-inch beam12 feet long. Because the beam was so long, I decided to use the contractor's checkout line. Contractors hate it when regular people, people who don't do this for a living, use this line. Nothing irks a contractor more than waiting in line with 15 bags of concrete behind some dope holding a few washers, or a broom, or, worst of all, a houseplant. But this time, I thought, I had an excuse. This beam was too large to maneuver through the regular lines. I took a deep breath and made my way over to the contractor's line.

Which is where I found a long line, held up by a well-dressed suburban couple buying, of all things, houseplants. One of the plants looked a little droopy, so the wife dispatched the husband to run back and grab a more healthy replacement. All while the rest of the line waited. And waited.

I looked around. All the other guys in line, clearly contractors, were shaking their heads in disgust. I glanced at the two guys behind me. "Can you believe those clowns," one said sarcastically over his cartload of roofing materials. "Like we got all day to sit while they get a prettier plant." The other nodded, looking to me. I nodded too.

Then it hit me. They thought I was one of them. I was in.

During the week, I wear a suit and tie. As a lawyer, I attempt to look distinguished and thoughtful. But this had been a long weekend, and I had been attempting to finish the deck before company came, and I was not myself. I had not showered in recent memory, was wearing dirty boots and work clothes, and was sporting a bright red sunburn. My clothes showed rips and stains from various home repair projects. The sunburn looked just like the kind contractors get from framing lumber all day in the hot sun. (Mine came from an afternoon of playing with the kids at the wave pool of a waterpark, but that was immaterial.)

We began to talk. We talked about how these megastores are OK, but they tempt "Joe Homeowners" to take on projects that are way beyond them. We talked about how it's tough to get in and out of here and back to work with all these goshdarn amateurs getting in the way of our stinking carts. (We did not, of course, use the words "goshdarn" or "stinking." We were tough guys, and we used language that can't be printed in the newspaper.) We talked about how people want everything done right away, and perfectly, but don't want to pay for skilled labor. It was like drinking testosterone on the rocks. The more we talked, the more I felt part of the group. And the guiltier I felt.

My new friends nodded at my cart full of pressure-treated wood. "Whatcha working on, buddy?" one asked.

"Ah" I snorted, "putting in a deck for some joker who doesn't know what he's doing." They all snorted, too, in sympathy. "What the heck is taking so flipping long?" I growled. (Again, it's not an exact transcript.)

Just then, at the worst possible time, my wife and daughters came in from the car, where'd they'd been waiting.

"Did you buy your wood, Daddy?" one of the girls asked. I tried to pretend I did not know who these people were.

"Wait here," my wife said, pushing the girls toward me. "I have to run to the back and get some string to tie up my tomato plants."

As my wife made her way to the back of the store, and the girls began to climb over the cart, I kept my eyes to the ground, not wanting to meet the disgusted and disappointed stares of my former comrades.

I didn't even look up as one of the girls explained, out of the blue "My Daddy's all red cause he didn't wear sun cream at the water park." I'd have to explain to her later that Daddy was red in the face for another reason.

Last- Minute Tree

My wife and I got our Christmas tree early again this year, the way we do every year. Maybe it's our love of the holiday or an attempt to get the most bang for our buck, but the tree goes up in early December and stays up straight through until sometime in mid-January, when we haul out its bare, dried-out skeleton for the trash men. Ours is usually the last one out, and neighbors kid us about why we pulled all the needles off before we discarded the poor thing. The only people who decorate earlier than we do are department stores.

But any time before Christmas Eve afternoon is early for me. I grew up in a house of nine children, and for various reasons, chief among them financial, my family waited until the last minute to get our tree.

As soon as my father got home from work on Christmas Eve, we'd all pile into the station wagon and head out for the tree lot. There, the ritual would begin. One by one, my father would examine the trees with a critical eye. Pulling off a few needles here, pointing out a bare spot there, he'd subtly let the tree salesman know that this was December 24, and that if we did not take the tree, it would probably still be there on Christmas morning, forgotten.

After waiting all day for Pop to come home, the smaller children, myself included, could barely contain ourselves. This was the tree!, we wanted to shout. It was beautiful! Our older brothers and sisters would hold us back, sometimes with hands over our mouths, anxiously waiting to see how far down Pop could drive the price. Some years, the bargaining would get tough, with Pop telling all of us to get back in the car, that we could easily go somewhere else.

In the end, though, we'd always get our tree. The salesman would relent, probably out of pity for a man with nine scraggly children tailing behind him. The whole ride home would be filled with excited stories about how well we'd done and how scared the salesman had looked that he might lose a sale.

At home, the four-foot-high box, lugged up from the basement and filled with Christmas lights and ornaments dating back to the Forties, would be waiting. Kerry, the oldest sister, would be in charge of carefully selecting ornaments from the box and handing them to the younger boys for placement on the tree, while other older siblings were in charge of rearranging those same ornaments to better spots while we weren't looking. Then would come the tinsel. I can still hear my sisters calling out "Don't clump! Don't clump!"

We'd clump anyway, knowing that those same siblings who had rearranged our ornaments would be waiting to take those clumps and spread them out across the tree neatly.

When the tinsel met with everyone's approval, we'd plug in the tree and turn out all the lights in the house. And there we would sit for at least a half an hour, just talking about how perfectly the tree turned out and what a great deal we'd gotten.

While I realize now that the tree, one of the few still left on the lot late on Christmas Eve, was probably in some way defective or lopsided, or simply ugly, it didn't matter. It was ours, and it was all the more beautiful because we had grabbed it, with Pop, just in the nick of time. I don't remember a huge amount about my childhood, but those memories are as vivid as if they had happened yesterday.

My own five kids will never know that tradition. Like most people, we go early, choose the biggest, fattest tree we can find, pay full price, and keep the tree up so long that we're sick of it in the end. But on Christmas Eve, coming home from last-minute shopping, I slow as I pass the tree lots, see the last few stragglers hoping to make it into a living room before midnight, and I remember.

What Goes Up…..

There's an old adage, really a law of nature, that says "what goes up must come down." Somehow, my house defies this rule, especially when it comes to holiday decorations.

By definition, holiday decorations are items that you put out shortly before a holiday, and then take down again shortly after the season ends. At our house, decorations go up and stay up until knocked down by an act of nature or vandalism.

This year, as always, I will overdo it. I will climb the ladder and put wreaths in each of the front windows of the house. I will thread garland through the picket fence, and I will decorate the fanlight over the front door with an arrangement of pineapples, oranges, and apples, as you might see on a traditional colonial home. We'll put out little ceramic houses with lighted windows, decorate our mantels with pine boughs and cones, and put out the manger set on the table by the fireplace.

The house will look, at least for a few weeks, like the Kringle residence. Then, in a flash, Christmas will come, wrapping paper will fly like a sudden snow squall, and before we know it, it will all be over.

Shortly after Christmas, I will begin the process of thinking about removing the decorations. Despite increasingly sharp reminders from my wife, and annoyed and bewildered looks from the neighbors, I will put off the work of taking down the decorations. While it is easy to muster up the Christmas spirit, I've found it's almost impossible to marshal up the post-Christmas cleanup spirit.

So the wreaths will stay on the windows, waiting for a big spring storm to come along and knock them off the house. The garland will disappear on its own some day in mid-February, stolen by a dog or perhaps by some neighbor who is just sick of looking at it. The fanlight fruit arrangement, quite festive during the cold Christmas snap, will begin to thaw out in warmer weather, and will slowly drip warm pineapple juice on the childrens' heads as they go out the door. Only then, after I notice that the children have begun smell like tropical drinks, will I get out the stepladder and remove it.

Retrieving and repacking Christmas decorations is easy to put off because it means work and aggravation. Last year, we couldn't put away the manger set until we located baby Jesus, a process that took three weeks, as the Christ Child had been "adopted" by our daughters' Barbies and had taken up residence in their dollhouse upstairs. We found him propped in a toy high chair in the dollhouse kitchen, waiting for breakfast.

But never taking down your Christmas decorations also has its advantages. We have a box holly out front that each Christmas we decorate with little white lights. Last year, as I went to string the lights, I found that the lights from the year before had never been taken off. I simply plugged in last year's lights and went back in the house, smug but a little embarrassed.

Visitors sometimes ask about the Christmas bulbs hanging from the windows in the living room. Years ago, when the children were small enough to toddle headlong into the Christmas tree, my wife hung the nicest ornaments from the curtain rods, something we saw in a home magazine. They are still there, looking appropriate in December but slightly odd the rest of the year.

I could put the best face on it, and try to give people the impression that my house is like one of those holiday theme stores you see it quaint little towns, where it always feels like Christmas, no matter what month of the year. That may be true, but it's not intentional. It's because I'm too lazy to drag the ladder out of the garage or lug the packing boxes out of the basement.

For me, the decorations are a little like post-Christmas credit-card bills. What seemed like so much fun, and such a good idea, in December will come back to haunt you well into the New Year.

You can stop by any time in January and February if you're looking for a little Christmas cheer. But if you do, make sure and put on a hat before you ring the doorbell. If you don't, you'll end up with pineapple juice in your hair.

The "Wall of Fame"

I grew up in a family where we took very few snapshots. As a matter of fact, I have no pictures at all of me as a baby. As a growing boy, this lack of baby pictures led me to a firm belief that I had originated in an orphanage instead of the same gene pool as my brothers and sisters. (This insecurity was of course encouraged by my older brother, who whispered to me regularly that I had been adopted after being found on the curb, the discarded, freakishly mutated spawn of a group of passing gypsies.) Having few snapshots of my own childhood, I saw little interest in photos at all, thinking the whole idea of family pictures a little odd.

My wife, on the other hand, grew up with a lot of family pictures, so many that she has trouble displaying them all around our house. (We actually have 38 framed photos displayed in our living room right now. I just counted.) With no more room on tables, radiators or shelves, she began to hang photos on the wall in our front hall. Soon, they spread up the stairs, around the first floor landing, and into the second floor hall.

For years, I saw my wife's "Wall of Fame," as she jokingly calls it, as little more than decoration. To me, the black and white photos looked like the wall of a restaurant where all the famous patrons were long dead. The pictures cover a couple of cracks in our plaster, and every once in a while, one would come crashing down the steps as a child ran by waving his or her arms (usually being chased by whatever brother or sister he or she had just hit). The only time I noticed the pictures was as I swept up broken glass while lecturing whoever caused the damage.

But one day earlier this year, I stopped as I came down the steps and looked at the faces on the wall. There was my wife's grandmother, caught in the act of laughing at some moment in the mid-'20s. Her smile, and the way that her eyes crinkled when she did so, looked so much like my wife's familiar smile that I was taken aback. As I moved from picture to picture, I began to see that these were not just stiff poses. They were people like us, holding up prize fish, relaxing on porches, attending parties. And each of these people had left a mark, in one way or another, that showed up in the faces of my wife, and my children, today.

So the next time I visited my oldest sister, the keeper of my family's history, I borrowed her scrapbooks containing the few family photos from my side of the family. As I flipped through the scrapbooks at home, I recognized pictures I hadn't seen in years. I remember looking at these snapshots when I was younger, amazed that the businessman in the horn-rimmed glasses who regularly yelled at me to clean my room had once been a soldier behind the lines in World War II. And my mother, whom I thought of mainly as the source of pot roast and clean socks, had once been photographed posing with a handsome friend who was on his way to Japan. When I asked about the photo, my mother told me to put it away and not mention it around my father. (The way this creepy guy had his arm around my mom, and his far too broad smile, made me a little uncomfortable.) But where as a boy I had experienced only surprise that my parents had ever been young, I now saw important clues as to where I had come from.

I took the family photo album and started a project to scan them into the computer and save them in electronic form, on CD, so they could be distributed among my brothers and sisters. A few of the pictures, though, I printed out immediately and framed, so I could add them to the "Wall of Fame." As I placed my family's pictures on the wall among my wife's, I realized that I had now reached the age where it becomes just as important to look back as it is to look forward.

Now, when I come down the steps in the morning, I see the faces of my mother and father, of my great-grandfather and his nine children, looking on. Although they peer through somewhat hazy copies, their faces are still recognizable to me.

Except, of course, the face of that somewhat creepy guy who went to Japan. Him, I still don't like.

EPILOGUE

In the introduction of this book, I included some heartfelt and mushy lines about how this book was really just written for me. I said I didn't care if you actually bought the book at all, as it contained *my* memories and would see me through my old age.

That was, of course, a complete lie. If you borrowed this book from someone else, stop being so cheap and buy one of your own. If you bought this book and liked it, buy one for a friend. If you *really* liked the book, buy a whole bunch of them and give them out as Christmas presents. If you got this book out of a library, take it back and buy your own copy.

Because my memories aren't going to mean as much if I have to treasure them in the poorhouse.